Designing to Avoid Disaster

Recent catastrophic events, such as the I-35W bridge collapse, New Orleans' flooding, the BP oil spill, Port-au-Prince's destruction by earthquake, Fukushima nuclear plant's devastation by tsunami, the Wall Street investment bank failures, and the housing foreclosure epidemic and the collapse of housing prices, all stem from what author Thomas Fisher calls *fracture-critical design*. This is design in which structures and systems have so little redundancy and so much interconnectedness and misguided efficiency that they fail completely if any one part does not perform as intended. If we, as architects, planners, engineers, and citizens, are to predict and prepare for the next disaster, we need to recognize this error in our thinking and to understand how design thinking provides us with a way to anticipate unintended failures and increase the resiliency of the world in which we live.

In *Designing to Avoid Disaster*, Fisher discusses the context and cultural assumptions that have led to a number of disasters worldwide, describing the nature of fracture-critical design and why it has become so prevalent. He traces the impact of fracture-critical thinking on everything from our economy and politics to our educational and infrastructure systems, to the communities, buildings, and products we inhabit and use every day. And he shows how the natural environment and the human population itself have both begun to move on a path toward a fracture-critical collapse that we need to do everything possible to avoid. We designed our way to such disasters and we can design our way out of them, with a number of possible solutions that Fisher provides.

Thomas Fisher is the dean and a professor of architecture at the College of Design at the University of Minnesota.

Designing to Avoid Disaster

The Nature of Fracture-Critical Design

THOMAS FISHER

Routledge
Taylor & Francis Group

NEW YORK AND LONDON

First published 2013
by Routledge
711 Third Avenue, New York, NY 10017

Simultaneously published in the UK
by Routledge
2 Park Square, Milton Park, Abingdon, Oxon OX14 4RN

*Routledge is an imprint of the Taylor & Francis Group, an informa
business*

Library of Congress Cataloging in Publication Data
Fisher, Thomas, 1953–
   Designing to avoid disaster : the nature of fracture-critical design /
   Thomas Fisher.
      pages cm
   Includes index.
   1. Design–Methodology. 2. Safety factor in engineering. I. Title.
   NK1520.F57 2012
   620.8'6–dc23   2011051098

ISBN: 978–0–415–52735–4 (hbk)
ISBN: 978–0–415–52736–1 (pbk)
ISBN: 978–0–203–11329–5 (ebk)

Typeset in Didot and Helvetica
by Keystroke, Station Road, Codsall, Wolverhampton

Acquisition Editor: Wendy Fuller
Project Manager: Laura Williamson
Production Editor: Kyle Duggan

Printed and bound in Great Britain by
TJ International Ltd, Padstow, Cornwall

Contents

Preface: Designed Catastrophes

As I write these words, the whole world watches and waits to hear the news from the Fukushima nuclear power plant, crippled by the tsunami that followed the major earthquake off the coast of northern Japan on March 11, 2011.[1] While the Japanese building codes had well prepared most structures to withstand the earthquake, the enormous death toll and damage caused by the subsequent tsunami revealed the vulnerability of that country—and most countries—in seismically active coastal zones. Seawalls meant to stop a tsunami along Japan's coast proved completely inadequate to the size and force of the wave that came ashore, sweeping away almost every person, object, and structure in its wake. Likewise, the Fukushima plant, perched on a low bluff above the ocean, had not been designed to withstand such a large tsunami, which destroyed the many backup systems that kept the nuclear fuel from melting down.

Some might call this catastrophe an act of nature, something that no one could have anticipated. But that hardly seems credible. We have long known that the more forceful an earthquake undersea, the greater the force of the tsunami that follows. What happened in Japan parallels other recent disasters, including the sinking of the Deepwater Horizon oil rig in the Gulf of Mexico in 2010, which led to the largest oil spill in U.S. history, many times larger than the 11-million-gallon spill of the *Exxon Valdez* oil tanker off the coast of Alaska in 1989.[2] And both of those events echo what remains the most expensive disaster in human history: the flooding of New Orleans after Hurricane Katrina, with the breeching of the levees surrounding the city in 2005.[3]

Nor have such catastrophes remained confined to infrastructure like power plants, oil rigs, or levees. A similar pattern has characterized collapses of another kind: the precipitous decline of housing prices in wake of the Great Recession and the dramatic fall of the Wall Street investment banks, Bear Sterns and Lehman Brothers, which helped trigger the implosion of the global financial industry widely blamed for bringing on the recession.

Disasters of other sorts have also unfolded in recent years: extreme weather events such as record-breaking temperatures, extended droughts, and severe storms that have killed people and animals, withered crops, dried up water supplies, and flattened buildings and whole communities. Meanwhile, large sections of Port-au-Prince, Haiti crumbled into rubble, killing some 230 people and rendering 2 million homeless as the result of poor construction that could not withstand the 2010 tremor that remains one of the most deadly on record.[4] While diverse in location and different in their cause, all of these catastrophes have their origin in a particular kind of design error that we have made repeatedly, especially since World War II, and that will continue to plague us until we understand it and take action to counter it before even more costly disasters occur.

Humans suffered catastrophes before World War II, of course. You could rightly argue that nothing we have experienced recently compares to the human disaster of the Black Death in medieval Europe, which killed anywhere from 30 to 60 percent of the population, or the annihilation of the Native American population in North America in the wake of European exploration and expansion, which killed an estimated 80 percent of the native people.[5] Nor have we witnessed anything like the catastrophe of 65 million years ago when an asteroid nearly six miles wide collided with the earth and so altered the global climate that an estimated 90 percent of the species on the planet went extinct.[6] Our recent disasters may be more expensive, in dollar amounts, simply because of the value of the assets affected by them. But we have not seen such massive loss of life. And yet, as we will see, the potential for mass deaths among humans has never been greater in modern times than it is now.

Such news may sound depressing and something most of us don't want to think about, particularly if we feel helpless to do anything about it. In the case of catastrophes in the past, that was largely true. The first five recorded mass extinctions on the planet, for example, all had natural causes. What distinguishes many of the disasters we have faced recently is that they have stemmed largely from design errors, from mistakes of our making. As such, they remain within our control, for if we designed our way into these disasters, we can design our way out of them. But we first have to understand the nature of our errors so that we don't simply repeat them, as we have been doing over and over in recent decades.

Some of the recent disasters stem from obvious human error, such as the poorly designed and maintained blow-out protection system that failed when the Deepwater Horizon caught fire in the Gulf or the badly designed and maintained levee system that led to the flooding of much of New Orleans or the inadequately designed and built concrete structures and squatter settlements in Port-au-Prince that collapsed during the earthquake or the vulnerable nuclear power plant in Japan not built to withstand the horizontal force of a tsunami. Other catastrophes, though, not often thought of in terms of human error, have their origin in bad design. The collapse of the banking system, for instance, stems from poorly conceived investment vehicles, so complicated that even the Wall Street bankers who devised and sold these products seem to have had little idea how much they had put their own institutions and the global economy at risk.[7] Likewise, the dramatic fall of housing prices in places like Florida and California had its origin in large-scale residential developments built there in recent decades, where the resale value of the nearly identical houses remains extremely vulnerable to deflation if enough homes go into foreclosure.[8]

Not only do we not see phenomena like the banking crisis or the collapse of housing prices as design related, but we also rarely see the connection between economic disasters like these and the physical and environmental ones that have occurred at the same time and, in places like the Gulf Coast, sometimes in the same general geographic area. By not seeing the catastrophes we now face as related and part of the same systemic problem, we also miss the opportunity to understand their underlying causes and the ability to predict their occurrence before they happen. That prediction is more than just an academic exercise. Given the number of people and other species affected by these catastrophes and the severity of their impact on lives and livelihoods, the prediction of disasters before they occur may be one of the most important tasks we face as a civilization and, indeed, as a species.

In the first part of this book, I will lay out the nature of the design errors that have generated so many of the disasters we have encountered in recent years. In doing so, I hope to show how we might spot these errors and take action to prevent them from turning into catastrophes. In the second section, I will show how these design errors occur in myriad parts of modern life and in aspects of our society and economy that have gone largely unrecognized, while posing an enormous threat to our future. After that, I will discuss the origin of such errors in the widespread misunderstanding of design in modern culture, which has led to the failure of so many of the systems that we depend on. I will then outline, in the third section of the book, ways of responding to this problem and correcting it in the future to reduce the likelihood of it happening again. I hope that, by the end, we will be able to see what a more resilient world, more resistant to catastrophic failure, might look like and how to prepare ourselves better for disasters when they do occur.

Acknowledgments

The core idea of this book first appeared as a chapter, "Fracture Critical: The I-35W Bridge Collapse," that I wrote for the book *The City, The River, The Bridge: Before and After the Minneapolis Bridge Collapse* (University of Minnesota Press, 2011), with parts of several chapters first appearing as editorials that I wrote for the ACSA News during my year as president of the Association of Collegiate Schools of Architecture. Parts of Chapters 4 and 5 also first appeared as an essay, "The Anti-Shock Doctrine of Design," in the journal of the Louisiana State University School of Architecture, *Batture* (vol. 4, 2008) and much of Chapter 33 first appeared as a foreword to the book *New Directions in Sustainable Design* (Routledge, 2011). Several other chapters began as talks I have given to a number of organizations and schools over a couple of years.

I want to thank the graduate student Kamana Dhakhwa, who redid the drawings and who helped get permissions for this book. I would also like to thank my wife and daughters—Claudia, Ann, and Ellen—for their patience as I wrote this book. They have shown what a resilient family can be like.

PART I

The Nature of Fracture-Critical Design

The Increasing Incidence of Disasters

It may seem hard enough to accept the idea that we have designed our way into many of the disasters that we have experienced of late, but harder still to accept that such disasters will likely occur with ever-greater frequency in the near future. The United Nations International Strategy for Disaster Reduction (ISDR) has data on global disasters, going back through records to 1900, with updated statistics through 2005.[1]

The increase in catastrophes, especially since World War II, is striking. After 1945, the incidence of disasters worldwide begins to move rapidly upward, with "hydrometeorological" events, such as droughts, floods, and storms, rising most noticeably: the number of weather-related catastrophes increased 400 times, by 2005, over the number of such disasters in 1900.[2] While such events remain "natural" occurrences in the minds of many, the overwhelming evidence of the scientific community points to human activity such as the burning of fossil fuel in buildings, industry, and vehicles as having prompted climate change and the more extreme weather-related disasters that accompany it. As climatologist Mark Seeley has put it: "The more energy we put into the atmosphere, the more energy it gives back to us."[3] In other words, the more we can reduce the emission of climate-changing greenhouse gases, the more we can begin to lessen the number and intensity of hydrometeorological disasters.

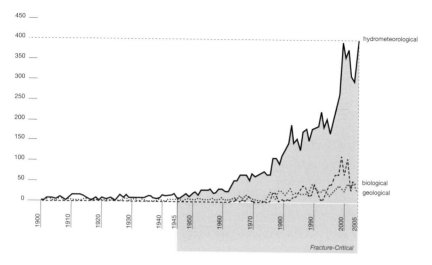

Figure 1.1 Number of natural disasters registered in EM-DAT (an Emergency Events Database maintained by CRED) across the years 1900–2005. While data gathering and record keeping related to weather-related disasters have improved, that alone cannot account for the rapid rise in the number of such events occurring around the world as our climate changes.

Biological disasters, such as epidemics and insect infestations, and geological disasters, such as earthquakes, tsunamis, and volcanic eruptions, have also increased about the same amount during the twentieth century, roughly to thirty to forty-five times the number in 1900. However, these two kinds of catastrophes have had different trajectories. Around the turn of the twenty-first century, the number of biological disasters spiked to over 100 times that of a century before, while geological disasters have never increased to more than fifty times the number in 1900.[4] Both of these types of disasters, however, have similar causes: populations living in closer proximity, in over-crowded, unsanitary conditions that can generate epidemic disease and on unstable ground in unstable buildings that remain vulnerable to the hazards of tremors and tsunamis. Here, too, we have designed—or rather badly designed—our way into such disasters. At the same time, we can greatly reduce the loss of life and cost of damage of biological and geological catastrophes by ensuring that all people live and work in safe and sanitary conditions.

These hazards do not occur uniformly around the globe. Obviously climates differ from one location to another, as do factors such as density of population and vulnerability to geological or climatological events. Some events, such as the post-Katrina flooding along the Gulf Coast in 2005 or the Kobe earthquake in Japan in 1995, outpace all the others in terms of cost, but remain relatively small percentages of the gross domestic products of the countries in which they occurred. Other events, such as the floods in Bangladesh in 2004 and those in North Korea in 1995, cost relatively little in absolute dollar amounts, but constituted a huge percentage of those nations' economies.[5] But, in the United States, those who think that disasters befall others need to think again.

The United States ranked third among countries most often hit by natural disasters and it leads the world in the cost of these events, with Katrina remaining the most expensive disaster to date, at an estimated $110 to $125 billion. And the United States alone absorbed over $365 billion dollars in disaster-related damages between 1991 and 2005, with only Japan and China coming close to that figure, and with the average cost of disasters in all other countries less than one-tenth as expensive.[6] And yet, while the United States exceeds others in the cost of disasters generally, disasters have different geographies. While epidemic disease has increased eightyfold over the twentieth century, for example, the distribution of such diseases remains highly uneven. The number of people killed by biological illness, for instance, was one-third more in the least developed countries than in developing nations and 160 times more than in the most developed parts of the world.[7]

Some could argue that the criteria used by the Centre for Research on the Epidemiology of Disasters (CRED) in reporting these findings have skewed the data. For example, CRED uses a rather narrow definition of what constitutes a disaster: a "situation or event, which overwhelms local capacity, necessitating a request to national or international level for external assistance; [and] an unforeseen and often sudden event that causes great damage, destruction and human suffering."[8] Such disasters get recorded if they meet at least one of the following criteria:

- ten or more people reported killed
- 100 people reported affected
- declaration of a state of emergency
- call for international assistance.

Considering the impact of disasters like the Katrina flooding or the Haitian earthquake, these criteria seem mild in comparison. But CRED has used these criteria consistently and so while someone might dispute the total number of disasters, the relationship between catastrophic events across the 105 years represented by the data remains the same. And as we will see, that relationship matters much more than absolute numbers.

At the same time, some might argue that changes in data gathering and reporting disasters have skewed the relationship among these events. Clearly, we have better data in recent decades because of the more reliable and consistent data gathering that digital tools and global communications allow. But, disasters rarely go entirely unnoticed, if only at a local level, and so we should trust the research that CRED and other organizations have done to ascertain, as accurately as possible, the incidence of catastrophes across the last century. To do otherwise would simply cloud the reality that we face as a human species: that the number of particularly weather-related disasters and the number of people on the planet since World War II have both grown exponentially.

That rate of growth is key, as we will see. Exponential growth has the paradoxical effect of lulling us into complacency because of the peculiar nature of such growth. When something increases exponentially, even a benign or beneficial situation can become unmanageable and even devastating quite quickly. In 1996, for example, the number of weather-related disasters reported worldwide that year stood at roughly 175, a seemingly modest amount and less than the number reported in 1984. But by 1999 the number of such disasters had climbed to around 400, an increase of over 200 percent in just three years.[9]

Human population numbers have increased even more alarmingly. In 1950, world population stood at about 2.5 billion people;

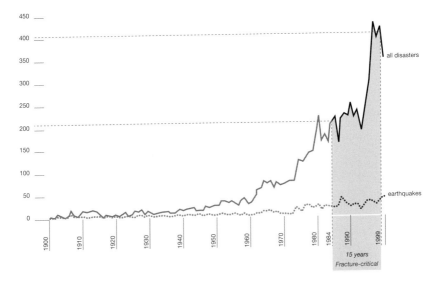

Figure 1.2 Trends in number of reported events. When comparing all disasters around the globe to the relatively stable incidence of earthquakes worldwide, we can see that the growing numbers of people living in hazard zones has greatly increased the number and severity of catastrophic events since the 1950s.

by 2005, it had increased to 6.5 billion, a 260 percent increase in a little more than half a century. By the end of 2010, the number stood at close to 7 billion.[10] That it took our entire history to reach 2.5 billion and less than the average lifetime of one person to grow 260 percent shows the nature of the complacency that such exponential increases can instill. Those in the most developed parts of the world may not see the population growing that quickly and so may think that we have time to adjust to having so many more people on the planet than just a generation or two ago, but exponential growth actually gives us very little time to respond. We have become, literally, a species out of control, and the disasters we face remind us of that. Floods, earthquakes, and plagues have occurred on the planet and among species long before humans ever evolved. But those events, combined with our excessively large numbers, make such "natural" events catastrophic in their effects on us.

And not just on us. The CRED data primarily focuses on the direct effects of disasters on humans, with little or no mention of its impact on plant and animal life. And yet, the diminishment or destruction of other species and the ecosystems upon which they thrive can have long-term consequences for us. The oil spill off the Louisiana coast barely makes one of the ISDR criteria: with eleven people killed this was just one more than the ten-person number needed to declare it a disaster. But the impact on sea life and on the wetlands and along the shorelines of the Gulf Coast has been absolutely catastrophic, not only for the millions of plants and animals killed by the spill, but for the millions of people affected by the loss of those ecosystems for generations to come.[11]

2

Our Planetary Ponzi Scheme

These disasters to both human populations and to other species have not happened by accident; we have designed a system to maximize the rewards of a relatively few people, while threatening most others on the planet. This system has worked well for those at the top, but it has negatively affected enough other people or species to undermine its stability—even for those at the top. And over the last few decades, the devastating consequences of this have become too large to ignore, with billions of people living in abject poverty and an accelerating rate of species extinctions underway. To understand what we have put in place, we might turn to a metaphor, one that recent events have made readily apparent: we have, since at least the industrial revolution over the last two centuries, engaged in a vast Ponzi scheme with the planet.

I first read of that idea on September 4, 2009 in an essay in *The Chronicle Review*, in which David Barash, a professor of psychology at the University of Washington, argued that "in our fundamental relationship to the natural world—which is, after all, the fundamental relationship for everyone—we are all Madoffs."[1] Barash referred to the over $50 billion Ponzi scheme that Bernard Madoff perpetrated on his investors, using the funds he received from new clients, lured by his claims of guaranteed high returns, to pay earlier investors the money that he had promised them. A Ponzi scheme holds enormous appeal to unscrupulous people. It can make its perpetrator, and its initial investors, fabulously wealthy. But as we have seen with Madoff's fraud, such schemes cannot last; eventually they run out of resources to keep feeding those at the top. As Barash points out, such "pyramid schemes are not sustainable. Eventually they fail. It isn't possible to keep recruiting a never-ending supply of suckers."[2]

Madoff, though, did us all a favor by demonstrating something that we hadn't recognized before. The original Charles Ponzi, who invented this form of fraud, had a scheme that lasted a matter of months in 1920 before it came crashing down. But Madoff did something Charles Ponzi could only dream of, realizing that if a Ponzi scheme becomes large enough and pervasive enough, it becomes—paradoxically—harder to see and more difficult to accept. In that sense, Madoff played upon an understandable aspect of human nature. Once we become dependent upon something and

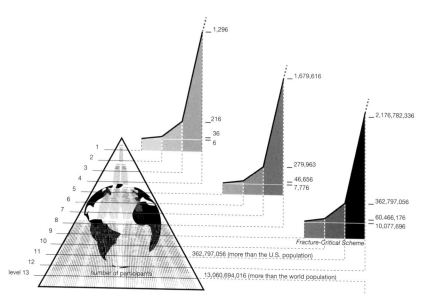

Figure 2.1 A Ponzi scheme like that pursued by Bernard Madoff has a fracture-critical nature because it requires exponentially increasing numbers of participants to keep it going and because it inevitably collapses, suddenly and often without warning.

have invested so heavily into it, we have every incentive to want to keep it going, even after we know it to be unsustainable. Some people had suspicions about Madoff and his promised returns on investments as too good to be true, but their warnings went unheeded because no one wanted to believe them.

Madoff's Ponzi scheme may go down in history as just another example of the financial fraud and unethical behavior that became all too common in an era in which capitalism has become "the worst enemy of humanity" as Bolivia's president, Evo Morales, has called it.[3] And to those of us who never invested with Madoff, his conniving may seem far from our concerns. But, as Barash suggests in his essay, when it comes to our treatment of the planet, "we are all Madoffs," or at least all participants in a Madoff-like pyramid scheme in which the wealthiest populations in the world pay themselves handsome returns by drawing down the available resources of the planet and inexpensive labor of poor people around the world.[4]

This has gone on for so long and become so enormous that we do not recognize the Ponzi-like nature of the global, industrial economy. Nor do we want to. Those of us living in developed nations have far too much at stake to want to see our standard of living come crashing down, and so we do what Madoff's investors must have done when warnings of a possible Ponzi scheme went public: we look the other way and don't want to know about it, in hopes that it isn't true. But it is true. The combination of modern technology and finance have enabled the last seven or eight generations of people to consume finite resources and exploit human labor at a rate never before seen in our past and no longer sustainable on into the future. We have, like all Ponzi schemes eventually do, run out of suckers, as Barash put it. It now takes 1.5 planets to meet the current needs of humans on our one globe, and with the base of our pyramid now larger than the world it stands on, the structures upon which we all now depend will become increasingly unstable and liable to sudden collapse.[5]

Barash asks this rhetorical question at the end of his essay: "Madoff eventually got 150 years in the slammer and worldwide derision. What's in store for the rest of us?"[6] What, indeed, lies in wait for the rest of us when the potential collapse we face doesn't just involve money, but fundamental aspects of human existence, such as a climate cool enough to grow the food we need to eat or to replenish the fresh water we need to live? Many will want to dismiss this Ponzi scheme metaphor as just that: a metaphor, a creation of our imagination and so not worth taking seriously. To which I would respond with Pascal's wager. Blaise Pascal, the seventeenth-century mathematician and theologian, argued that we cannot know if God exists or not, but that we would be wise to wager that he does, for if he doesn't exist and we bet that he does, we have lost nothing, but if he does exist and we bet that he doesn't, we have lost everything.[7]

The same argument applies to our Ponzi scheme with the planet. If Barash's metaphor is wrong and we bet that it is right, we have lost nothing. If, for example, we reduce our use of fossil fuels, curb our use of fresh water, limit our generation of greenhouse gases, and generally try to live in more ecologically friendly and more socially just ways, we will continue to live fulfilling lives — and healthier lives in the process. But, if Barash's metaphor is right and we bet he is wrong, we stand to lose everything. Like life without God to the religiously minded, we cannot maintain human civilization without adequate resources or sustain human life without enough food or fresh water. And if Barash's metaphor is right, those in the wealthiest countries also have the most to worry about. As the collapse of Madoff's Ponzi scheme showed, the largest investors in his fraud lost the most money, and the same will happen when our Ponzi scheme with the planet implodes. Those who have the most wealth now, with the most invested in the scheme as it has evolved since the industrial revolution, will have the farthest to fall and the most to lose.

That runs counter to what many people might want to wager. It may seem logical to assume that those who have the most have more of a cushion should resources become scarce, and more money to buy what they need if prices for food or fuel begin to skyrocket. But such a logic rests on the assumption that the world as we know it will continue to function as it has. Madoff's Ponzi scheme demonstrated that just the opposite occurs. When his pyramid scheme failed, his investors discovered nothing there, no pot of money from which they could recoup at least some of their losses. A Ponzi scheme works by continually fueling the fraud with new infusions of resources, with the perpetrators skimming off profits, but without setting aside any assets in case of a collapse. The same has happened with our planetary Ponzi scheme. We have exhausted resources, exploited people, and extinguished species with woefully inadequate stores set aside should the system implode. Those who assume that their current wealth will serve them well in a post-Ponzi-scheme world will find themselves as much at a loss as Madoff's biggest investors.

The way to survive such a collapse—and thrive afterward—depends upon understanding the nature and extent of the Ponzi scheme we have engaged in, and creating a life for others and ourselves that does not depend upon a fraudulent relationship with the planet. Humans have lived in more honest and equitable ways in the past and we can learn to live in those ways again. That will demand, though, a redesign of almost every system and structure that we have created over the past several generations in order to withstand the shocks and disasters that will continue to come our way as we come off the over-leveraged high we have had over the last century or two. And the sooner we get on with this, the better our chances of having a flourishing future.

3

Fracture-Critical Design

A Ponzi scheme such as Madoff's has what engineers call a "fracture-critical" structure. To understand what that means, look at what happened on August 1, 2007, when the fracture-critical 1,907-foot I-35W Bridge near downtown Minneapolis suddenly fell into the Mississippi River, killing thirteen people, injuring 145 more, severing a key link in the interstate transportation system, and costing over $300 million in damages and in the building of a new bridge.[1]

After over a year of investigating the possible causes of the collapse, the National Transportation Safety Board concluded that the engineers who designed the bridge in the early 1960s had undersized the gusset plates that connected the segments of the bridge's steel. That error, compounded by the weight added to the bridge over time with extra lanes, heavier vehicles, and additional repaving equipment and materials on the day of the collapse, led to the failure of the span. In a matter of a few seconds, 456 feet of the bridge fell 108 feet into the river, taking with it 111 vehicles.[2]

Experts estimate that some 465 bridges in the United States have designs similar to that of the I-35W span, and the inspection and reinforcement of those structures has become vitally important as this country embarks on a nationwide upgrading of its infrastructure. However, we need to see the I-35W Bridge and all of the other spans like it not as an isolated issue, having to do just with bridge design in the post-World War II period, but instead as part of a much

---

Figure 3.1 The collapse of the I-35W Bridge near downtown Minneapolis represented not just the failure of one bridge. It symbolized the fracture-critical nature of much of the infrastructure that has been put in place in the United States after World War II.

wider problem that characterizes much of the infrastructure and development that we have put in place over the last sixty years: fracture-critical design.

When engineers define a structure as fracture-critical, they refer to its susceptibility to complete and sudden collapse should any part of it fail. A fracture-critical design has four key characteristics, the first of which is a lack of redundancy. The undersized gusset plates on the I-35W Bridge might not have brought the entire span down if the bridge had enough redundant structural members to carry the load, even if some part of a truss failed. At the time of the bridge's design in the early 1960s, such a redundant structure might have seemed unnecessarily expensive and wasteful. However, given the extraordinary expense of replacing the entire bridge after its complete collapse, the relatively small incremental increase in cost of adding redundant structural members at the time of its initial construction would have been much more cost-effective. Bridge designers now understand that, and over the last few decades they have increased the redundancy of bridges, but the pressure to keep initial costs low remains a constant threat to the resiliency of our infrastructure.

The potential for the sudden failure of fracture-critical designs also comes from another feature of such systems: their interconnectedness and efficiency. The I-35W Bridge had both. When the gusset plates cracked near the southern end of the bridge, that rupture led to the cascading failure of other gusset plates and truss members, all of which were interconnected as part of a single structure in such an efficient design that nothing could interrupt the serial collapse. The 10th Avenue Bridge adjacent to the I-35W Bridge shows what a less interconnected and less efficient design entails. Completed in 1929, the 10th Avenue Bridge has several independent concrete arches, separated by large concrete pylons that divide the structure into discrete parts. At the same time, the myriad concrete columns supporting the road deck all seem oversized for the load they carry, making the entire ensemble less than efficient, but more than sufficient to compensate for the failure of any one element. Even if a number of columns or one of the arches were to fail, the entire bridge would not fall, given its division into independent sections and its redundant structural design.

A final characteristic of fracture-critical systems lies in their sensitivity to exponential stress on any one part. Had inspectors attached strain gauges to the gusset plates on the I-35W Bridge before it collapsed, they would have seen a gradual increase in stress on the plates, with a rapid rise in the strain on them just before the plates fractured and the bridge fell. That sudden, exponential increase in the strain in a structure prior to failure is a well-known phenomenon, but a fracture-critical design magnifies its effect. What may seem like a contained or controllable problem in one element can quickly become catastrophic, because of the peculiar nature of exponential growth, doubling with each increment of time. The danger of such exponential growth lies not only in the system itself, with its rapidly accelerating stress, but also in our thinking that we have plenty of time and adequate reserves in such situations, just before the window of opportunity to respond swiftly closes.

To understand how these characteristics of redundancy, connectedness, efficiency, and exponential change relate to each other, look at the concept of "panarchy," explored in a book by that name edited by the ecologists Lance Gunderson and C.S. Holling. Panarchy describes the way in which human and natural systems move in continuous adaptive cycles, where exponential growth in the

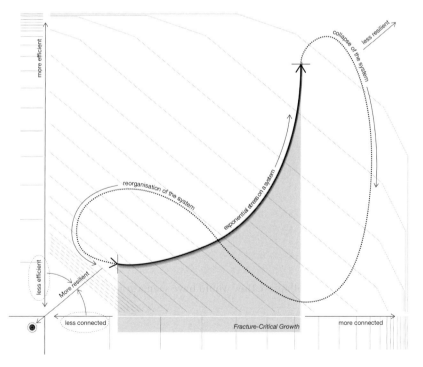

Figure 3.2 As in nature's ecosystems, human-designed systems can become so efficient and productive that they can no longer adapt to external or unexpected stresses, causing them to collapse back to a state of less efficiency, but greater diversity and resilience.

connectedness and efficiency within a system eventually makes it less and less resilient, leading eventually to its collapse back to a state of greater resilience, with fewer connections and less efficiency.[3] Fracture-critical designs like the I-35W Bridge represent the height of connectedness and efficiency, with the least amount of resiliency, and their collapse tells us, if we understand this as an adaptive cycle, that we need to replace them with systems that have greater resilience and less connectedness and efficiency.

We need to recognize, in other words, that our species itself has become fracture critical. As we have been destroying the habitat for so many other species, rendering them extinct at rates never before seen during human history, we have also been overstressing the natural systems upon which we, ourselves, depend for our survival. Most of us don't recognize the danger we are in, any more than those driving over or working on the I-35W Bridge recognized the danger they were in seconds before it fell. Indeed, the apparent strength and invincibility of the systems and structures we have designed to support our civilization can blind us to our vulnerability, as the sheer size and scale of the I-35W Bridge seemed to blind its inspectors to its liability to sudden collapse. But, as happened with that bridge, so too with our civilization: the higher and mightier we have become, the farther and faster we can fall.

We don't have to look far to envision a less fracture-critical future for ourselves. Humans have long lived in more resilient and sustainable ways, husbanding finite resources to ensure that future generations have enough, cultivating renewable resources to maintain their quantity and diversity, allocating desirable resources in ways that prevent over-consumption, and encouraging the enjoyment of infinite resources such as human community, creativity, and empathy. In material terms, this means a radical reduction in the quantity of the things we have, the spaces we inhabit, and the distances we travel, with a comparative and equally dramatic increase in the qualities of what we have, what we share with others, and what we hand down to our progeny. Like most of our ancestors, whose physical environment remained extremely modest and constrained in comparison to modern life, we will need to return to living within our environmental means as a species, which will involve considerably less material abundance than in recent generations, given the greatly increased numbers of us on the planet. But with those material constraints will come a rise in other forms of abundance—via families and friends, colleagues and communities—that we have tended to overlook in a culture and economy that has often over-emphasized the pursuit of personal prosperity.

That will not be easy for those of us who measure progress in terms of our profligacy. To them, the reduced quantities in our lives will seem like loss, and no doubt many people who have prospered from our domination of the planet will do all they can to resist any change, but we cannot let their fear dissuade us from doing what we need to do in order to preserve ourselves and to survive. If we can get past the hurdle of fear and resistance, however, we will find that the past gives us plenty of precedents from which to choose. Human societies and settlements have proven most resilient—and least fracture critical—when they have lived in units small enough to induce a sense of its members' responsibility for each other, while remaining relatively autonomous and depending largely upon local production and consumption of goods and services.

The structure that replaced the I-35W Bridge might also serve us as a guide here. Unlike its fracture-critical predecessor, the new bridge represents, metaphorically, the kind of change we will need to enact in much of the infrastructure we have put in place over the last half-century or more. First, the new bridge, designed by Linda Figg of Figg bridge engineers, has an extraordinary amount of redundancy in it. The sheer size and depth of the new bridge's post-tensioned, concrete box beams not only compensates for the weakness of the previous bridge, but also recognizes that it is ultimately better to build well at the beginning than to rebuild, at a much greater expense later on, after something has failed. Shortsighted efficiency at the start can lead to extraordinary costs in the end.

Second, the new bridge has great resiliency designed into it. It stands, for example, as essentially two bridges, side by side, without a physical link between the two over the river, so that even if one side fails for some unlikely reason, the other would remain intact and still functional. Creating disconnected and discrete parts within a system remains one of the best ways to ensure the survivability of the whole. The new bridge will also accommodate multi-modes of transportation, with some lanes strengthened to support future light-rail transit and with a pedestrian bridge planned for suspension beneath the highway span. The greater the number of alternatives a system can provide for, the greater the likelihood that it will endure.

Finally, the new bridge arose out of local conditions. Those conditions ranged from the specifics of the site, in which the closed-off highway on one end of the bridge became the construction yard for the new structure, to the specific concerns of the community, in which local decision-makers and the community at large had opportunities to give extensive input to the bridge's designers. The bridge also involved hundreds of local construction workers and materials suppliers, showing how much investment in better infrastructure amounts to one of the best ways to encourage economic activity, not only in the short term through job creation, but over the long term through higher productivity and greater security within a community.

If the new I-35W Bridge indicates what a fracture-resistant infrastructure might be like, it also shows how much a more resilient future will look a lot like what we have known in the past. The new bridge, for instance, uses the same material—reinforced concrete—and has a similar mass to the adjacent, eighty-year-old 10th Avenue Bridge. While the new bridge employs new techniques, like post-tensioning and prefabrication, that hadn't yet been widely developed in 1929, the two resilient structures have more in common than the new bridge has with its immediate fracture-critical predecessor.

That will likely be true of most of the infrastructure that we need to build or rebuild in the next fifty years. Our future will look more like our more distant past than it will the science-fiction fantasies that we have pursued since World War II, resulting in the fracture-critical circumstances that the planet and its people can no longer sustain. Over the coming decades, we need, instead, to bring together all of the environmental knowledge we have about nurturing the natural systems that we depend on, with all of the ethical understanding we can muster to help us thrive within the material constraints we will face. Of the bridges we will need to build in the process, the psychological bridge that helps us leave behind our old hubris in order to reach a newfound humility may be one of the most important of all.

Disasters on Demand

4

One of the biggest challenges we face in redesigning the fracture-critical systems and structures upon which we now depend lies in the fact that many powerful groups benefit from the way things currently exist and they believe that they will continue to do so if things collapse. Like hedge-fund investors who profit if the market goes up or down, the moral hazard in such a system reveals the perverse nature of the economics and politics of our time. Both the private and public sectors have helped create our Ponzi-like, fracture-critical world, and many players in both sectors seem to believe, falsely, that they can prosper on both sides of the equation.

Naomi Klein has dubbed this "disaster capitalism" in her book *The Shock Doctrine: The Rise of Disaster Capitalism*. In it, she shows how recent efforts to privatize the public sector have led to the perverse situation in which governments such as that of the United States under George W. Bush can create highly profitable conditions for especially large corporations by minimally regulating them and by commissioning them to clean up those same situations if things disastrously fail. As Klein writes:

The military-industrial complex that Dwight D. Eisenhower warned against in 1961 has expanded and morphed into what is best understood as a disaster-capitalism complex, in which all conflict- and disaster-related functions (waging war, securing borders, spying on citizens, rebuilding cities, treating traumatized soldiers) can be performed by corporations at a profit . . . it aims, ultimately, to replace core functions of government with its own profitable enterprises.[1]

Klein's book traces the rise of the shock doctrine to the "fundamentalist version of capitalism" promoted by the University of Chicago economist Milton Friedman who argued that "only a crisis — actual or perceived — produces real change," which for Friedman and his followers involved a radical diminishing of the public sector through "a rapid-fire transformation of the economy — tax cuts, free trade, privatized services, cuts to social spending and deregulation" in times of stress.[2]

Klein's compelling thesis seems, at first, outrageous, until we begin to contemplate the disasters that have occurred in recent years. Klein refers in her book to events such as Pinochet's coup in Chile in 1973, the Falklands War in 1982, the Tiananmen Square Massacre in 1989, the collapse of the Soviet Union in 1991, the Asian Financial crisis in 1997, and Hurricane Mitch in 1998. But the list goes on, as we know from recent experience. The public- and private-sector beneficiaries of the disaster-capitalism complex will never admit that they intended these failures to occur, any more than the instigators of a Ponzi scheme would ever admit that in the midst of building the fraudulent pyramid they intended it to collapse. But that does not mean that we should hold them harmless for the fracture-critical designs they have put in place. There are many more Madoffs among us who have yet to pay the price for what they have perpetrated on us.

Most people no doubt find it distressing to think of our government, in conjunction with our major corporations, manufacturing disasters as a form of economic development, while largely ignoring the pain, suffering, damage, and death that accompanies human-created catastrophes. Most of us go to work or go about our business each day trying to make the world a bit better, trying to raise a child, help a friend, serve a customer, aid a client, or advance an organization or agency in some small way. As human beings, we want to build, not destroy.

And when things don't work out, we like to attribute them to "natural causes" or describe them as "acts of God," unwilling to acknowledge that catastrophes often have human selfishness and self-interest somewhere in the chain of events leading up to them. Look at some of the most famous disasters in U.S. history: the 1871 Chicago fire and the 1906 San Francisco earthquake and fire.[3] While neither occurred intentionally—the one resulting from an accidentally set fire and the other the result of an almost eight magnitude earthquake—the extent of the damage, with flames leveling much of their city centers, revealed a high degree of self-interested neglect preceding both disasters. Both cities had a majority of buildings constructed of wood, set in close proximity, with inadequate fire-suppression systems—designed, in other words, to maximize the profit of owners and developers as the cities went up, and affording a maximum of profit to those who came in after the conflagrations to rebuild them.

It may seem unfair to assign blame to those who constructed Chicago and San Francisco before their respective fires. Building and zoning codes in the nineteenth and early twentieth centuries were rudimentary compared to today's standards, and most people in those places no doubt followed the common practices of the day when it came to developing a city. But both the Chicago and the San Francisco disasters suggest that Klein's disaster capitalism has gone on for a long time, long before the likes of Milton Friedman. Large-scale, urban calamities, followed by massive rebuilding efforts, date back to our earliest cities—places like ancient Troy—in which new cities arose on top of the charred remains of earlier ones.

There even exist arguments for the advantages of such periodic destruction and renewal. "Creative destruction," as the sociologist Werner Sombart called it, sees in disasters the potential for innovation and creativity to take hold and flourish.[4] The aftermath of the Chicago fire, for example, gave rise to the so-called Chicago School of architecture and the emergence of creative talents such as Louis Sullivan and Frank Lloyd Wright, who, along with a group of their architecture and engineering colleagues, developed steel framing methods and fireproof construction techniques that enabled the modern skyscraper to emerge as a building type that now exists worldwide.

Disasters, in other words, can lead to technical advances as well as personal adversity. They can also lead to new kinds of communities, as we will discuss at the end of this book. Good often comes with the bad, so that, in the case of post-fire Chicago and San Francisco, their large-scale devastation spawned stricter building and zoning codes as well as more economic activity. Disaster capitalism may promote privatization in the short term, as Klein argues, but if history is any guide, it also prompts more government regulation over the long term, defeating its supposed purpose of shrinking the public sector. That legacy of the shock doctrine may, in other words, be just the opposite of what its proponents intend.

Other paradoxes in the shock doctrine exist as well, apparent in the flooding of New Orleans after Hurricane Katrina. A clue occurs in Klein's observation that:

> Politicians have been free to cut taxes and rail against big government even as their constituents drove on, studied in, and drank from the huge public-works projects of the 1930s and 1940s. But after a few decades, that trick stops working. The American Society of Civil Engineers has warned that the United States has fallen so far behind in maintaining its public infrastructure — roads, bridges, schools, dams — that it would take more than a trillion and a half dollars over five years to bring it back up to standard. This past summer those statistics came to life: collapsing bridges, flooding subways, exploding steam pipes, and the still-unfolding tragedy that began when New Orleans's levees broke.[5]

Those broken levees, and the resulting flooding of New Orleans, had many of the characteristics of previous disasters: public negligence, underinvestment in infrastructure, a lack of preparedness. But, at least so far, the New Orleans' situation has differed significantly from what happened in Chicago and San Francisco after their fires. In the latter, rebuilding occurred almost immediately and energetically. In many of the flooded areas of New Orleans, rebuilding has been sluggish at best, with much of it occurring at the hands of volunteer groups such as Habitat for Humanity and various education-based organizations.

One paradox here is that privatization requires public aid in order to occur. Without confidence in the ability of the government to ensure that the levees will not fail again, investors have not rushed to rebuild, especially in the lowest-lying areas of the city. Here is where the neo-conservatives "railing against big government" — even when they are in control of the government — become truly self-defeating. By not investing in public infrastructure, government officials who seem almost irrational in their opposition to taxation preclude the very possibility of privatization by making rebuilding efforts too risky financially. Disaster capitalism, ironically, may turn out to be a true disaster for capitalism.

Another paradox lies in the danger disaster capitalism presents for those who seek to profit the most by it, either financially or politically. Like the initiators of a Ponzi scheme, who invariably end up destitute and in prison, disaster capitalism seems, eventually, to backfire on those who engage in it, leading to their ousting from public office or their incarceration on corruption charges. Look at what happened to Enron, the energy company that intentionally created blackouts in some of the cities they served in order to hike up the price of electricity and jack up their profits: it went bankrupt, its employees lost their jobs, and some of its leadership went to prison.[6] The company, taking advantage of the fracture-critical electrical infrastructure in this country, turned out to have a fracture-critical nature itself, collapsing suddenly once its fraud became public. Such disaster capitalism seems like a kind of Russian roulette: companies and municipalities taking advantage of inadequate or under-funded infrastructure while hoping to avoid the bullet that comes with engaging in such irresponsible behavior. As often happens with roulette, the players bring on their own end.

5

The Anti-Shock Doctrine

Why have we brought such disaster upon ourselves? How do otherwise seemingly intelligent people engage in such self-destructive activities? Psychologists Nathan DeWall and Roy Baumeister have argued that "we have an inbuilt psychological immune system that works tirelessly beneath our conscious awareness, tuning our mind to a more positive channel whenever we think about death." In their article in the journal *Psychological Science*, DeWall and Baumeister recount how they asked students to think about their own death and then what they thought of when presented with incomplete words like "jo_." Those who had just contemplated their death were much more likely to think of a positive word like "joy" than those students not asked to think about death beforehand. The latter tended to see neutral words like "job" or "jog."[1]

This suggests a somewhat perverse fascination with the worst that can happen, in order to feel good about our surviving it. That, of course, assumes we will survive. One of the characteristics of the disasters we now dabble in and the catastrophes we now court is their utter destructiveness; no longer just about a city burning or flooding or crumbling, the Ponzi scheme we have perpetrated has potential planetary effects, disrupting vital ecosystems upon which we depend as a species or climate conditions that have underpinned our very civilization. Perhaps deliberating on disasters of such scope and at such a scale makes us think about the joy of avoiding them even more intensely, but to actually do so will require a much greater rethinking of what constitutes a good life. It will likely need to be much more about giving and much less about getting, much more about cooperation and much less about competition, much more about contemplation and much less about consumption.

If nothing else, it will involve us all participating much more than many of us have in the past in cleaning up after the disasters we have brought upon ourselves and in repairing the damage they have caused. This has already begun to happen in a major way. A remarkable number of people of diverse ages and backgrounds, from college students to construction workers to middle-aged church members, flocked to New Orleans to help in its clean up and rebuilding.[2] The optimism and enthusiasm of those volunteers, surrounded by the extraordinary devastation brought on by the flood, recalls one of the most surprising aspects of the research into happiness that has begun to occur in the psychological community. We often feel happy when we can help others in need. Rather than get depressed by or despondent about a disaster, those who actively engage in rebuilding after a disaster often talk about the trans- formative and energizing nature of the experience — perhaps another indication of the psychological immune system that DeWall and Baumeister have identified.

How might disaster capitalism, then, also serve, paradoxically, as a way of immunizing ourselves from disaster? The media knows full well how much its readers and viewers find disasters fascinating, evident in the amount of time and space newscasters and editors devote to events such as plane crashes, bridge collapses, and the myriad catastrophes that occur. Like those students asked to con- template their own deaths, we seem to find an equally cathartic experience in contemplating the misfortune of others, and perhaps of ourselves, were we in the same situation.

It is, of course, one thing to contemplate disaster and another to bring it on intentionally. The latter represents the ethically objectionable act of endangering others in order to profit oneself, as if we were, on an individual level, sacrificing others in order to

Figure 5.1 How we respond to disasters says a lot about our ability to recover from them. After Katrina, the enormous outpouring of volunteer help, in contrast to the often-incompetent federal government efforts, shows how resiliency arises from myriad, small-scale actions more than from a few, large-scale ones.

trigger our own immune system. That the neo-conservatives who have engaged in disaster capitalism also try to claim the moral high ground on various social issues makes their position seem like the height of hypocrisy. Defending unborn fetuses while shrugging off the loss of life that comes with disaster capitalism represents a moral corruption of monumental proportion.

Can we turn disaster capitalism on its head and, instead of suffering with the results of its consequences, help imagine disaster before it occurs and thus immunize ourselves from it? Can we walk away from the global Ponzi scheme and instead of pretending it doesn't exist, start to define a good life as one lived within the resources reasonably available to us? And can we end our dependence on the fracture-critical systems we have put in place over the last several generations and, instead of ignoring their vulnerability to collapse, begin to put in place redundancies on the assumption that if a system can fail, it will? Such questions confront us all in the opening decades of the twenty-first century and our answers to them will determine whether or not the decades ahead of us bring renewal—or renewed disasters, each more costly and catastrophic than the last.

The design community has already headed down this path. If we designed our way into the disasters we have increasingly suffered from, we can design our way out of them just as well. One example of this is the Designmatters program at the Art Center College of Design in Pasadena, California, which uses design as a way of informing the public about the dangers they face if action is not taken to prepare for the earthquake that will inevitably hit the L.A. area.[3] The Los Angeles Earthquake Project arose out of the sense, according to former Art Center College president Richard Koshalek, that the politicians in the region had not adequately prepared the public for the coming catastrophe. Designmatters developed a multi-media effort to inform residents about the potential disaster that awaits them and to create "new models for readiness and community interaction in Southern California." While the impending and potentially catastrophic nature of a major earthquake in Los Angeles gives this work a particular urgency, the Los Angeles Earthquake Project also serves as a model for what educators and professionals could do to prepare people for disasters before they happen.

The project participants developed a promotional campaign—"The Los Angeles Earthquake: Get Ready"—that uses the marketing strategies of commerce to "sell" people on the dangers of disaster, deploying various media to get the public's attention amidst all of the other distractions in their lives.[4] A multi-volume sourcebook delivers the content that people will need to know in order to get ready, with top-quality graphics to make the information as accessible as possible. The project also calls for a highly visible and well-publicized civic event, drawing on the methods of Hollywood to stage a gathering that combines information and entertainment, to drive home the idea that people will need collective action in order to prepare for what lies ahead.

The earthquake that will one day hit L.A. will, of course, be a natural disaster, even though most of the injuries and deaths that it causes will come from buildings that collapse or burn. But the L.A. Earthquake Project suggests ways in which we can begin to develop antidotes to disaster capitalism. Before the politicians let the infrastructure deteriorate to the point of failure, before the predatory companies swoop in to privatize public sector activities, and before a pacified public gives over its rights in a moment of desperation, the project shows how we might spur defensive strategies by revealing the consequences of the shock doctrine before the shock comes. A well-designed anti-disaster campaign can put pressure upon those in power who procrastinate in investing in public infrastructure in order to create the conditions amenable to the profiteering of a few at the expense of the many.

Another example of countering disaster capitalism is Architecture 2030, an effort led by architect Edward Mazria to show the dire consequences of our not curbing the human generation of greenhouse gases.[5] His organization has created a series of web-based aerial maps of coastal communities showing the effect of rising seas on shoreline cities as a result of global climate change, entitled "Nation Under Siege, Sea Level Rise at Our Doorstep." Mazria has shown how a small group, with relatively little money and visibility, can transform the political dialogue as a result of helping people see the impact of their actions. Within a few months of the release of these images, Congress had already proposed adopting the aspiration of having federal buildings all meet the goal of zero carbon generation by the year 2030. Mazria's group used readily available information in the construction of their coastal flooding maps, something that the public sector could easily have done. But it took Mazria's imagination and his staff's visual communication skills to translate that data into a form that the public and politicians could see and understand.

Imagine what might have changed had such efforts occurred in New Orleans years ago, when we still had time to strengthen the levees, restore the delta's wetlands, and educate people about how to survive a flood. Information about this existed in various documents, although clearly it didn't mobilize public opinion sufficiently to force the government to act. Would it have made a difference if every resident in New Orleans saw the direct effect on their property of levee failures, the height of water in their houses, the damage to property, and the likely deaths of people? Might the rhetoric of no new taxes that underpins disaster capitalism have had less appeal had we tallied up the true post-disaster costs to taxpayers, far greater than any incremental investment would have been?

Some professionals may not feel comfortable in what may seem like political advocacy. Professionals have become accustomed to remaining politically neutral, turning themselves into what Thomas Hobbes called an "artificial person," suppressing their own personal positions in order to serve their clients.[6] As a result, most professional practice has become a largely passive process, in which professionals address problems that others create or define. This does not present a problem when people legitimately try to do the right thing and end up in trouble or in need. But in the case of disaster capitalism, when entities in the private or public sector instigate disasters that affect large numbers of people, the political neutrality and passive practices of many professionals becomes part of the problem. It renders the professional community, which remains a major force looking after the public good, largely powerless in using their knowledge and skill on behalf of public education and political change. Disaster capitalists have most of the professional community right where they want them.

Professionals and the general public alike do not have to accept this powerlessness, however. Pre-empting disasters by provoking political discussion and public action might anger some companies that have profited or benefited immensely from disasters. But as Klein's book suggests, the real annoyance might come from the public sector—ironically, since the government has the primary responsibility for emergency preparedness.[7] All too often, the very information that could prepare people about impending disasters remains buried in technical reports and couched in bureaucratic language, as if public agencies did not want to worry people or, more likely, bring pressure on politicians and policy-makers to act to prevent disasters from happening. Warnings about almost every one of the disasters already mentioned, from the Gulf oil spill to the I-35W Bridge collapse to the investment bank failures to the bursting of the housing bubble, existed in documents or reports, some of them publicly available. Unless we make them visible and emphasize the consequences of inaction, however, no amount of dry documentation will matter very much. The "shock doctrine" needs an anti-shock doctrine to inoculate us against the predators waiting to pounce upon our misfortune.

Activism on the part of professionals will require a new kind of pre-emptive practice that might involve two twists on the typical competition for work. First, all professions will need to take a more active role, in partnership with public interest groups, in helping define and identify problems before they occur rather than just reacting to the problems that others define to benefit their own interest. As a model, we might look to the public health profession and to the preventive-care aspects of medicine that work to prevent illness or disease from occurring in the first place rather than treating it after the fact. Such pre-emptive practices would, in a wide range of fields, play out the worst-case scenarios in a world increasingly plagued by disasters and help us take precautionary measures before those worst cases can happen, while demanding the regulation of the most predatory companies and the ousting of their political cronies.

At first, there may exist relatively little funding for such work, since we have an economy that prospers when "big things" happen, even if bad for us, rather than when nothing happens, even if good. However as we begin to realize the larger losses that can come in the wake of disasters and the number of communities and industries harmed by such events, in comparison to the relatively few vulture-like businesses that benefit from them, we will start to see the financial support for this work grow. Even now, the economic arguments should seem almost self-evident. Compared to the billions of dollars lost in the fishing and tourism industries along the Gulf Coast, would we still call it "socialism" to have a more regulated oil industry required to put in many more fail-safe mechanisms, safety inspections, and precautionary procedures on oil rigs, which would have cost infinitesimally as much? Such requirements are not anti-capitalism; they're just anti-disaster capitalism.

Second, such "anti-shock" work will often demand the involvement of a greater diversity of disciplines than the typical professional group engages. Instead of having almost everyone involved in an effort coming from the same field or set of disciplines, with the same blinders on, an anti-disaster collaboration may require a much wider range of people actively involved in pre-emptive work from the very beginning. Both the L.A. Earthquake Project and Architecture 2030 engaged a range of fields in order to base their work on the best available knowledge and to convey it in the most compelling way. These interdisciplinary teams do not just need scientists and engineers, but storytellers and visual communicators, community organizers and cultural anthropologists, public health physicians and public policy analysts. By seeing fracture-critical design as solely the concern of government inspectors and civil engineers, we have missed the larger problem created by such design and overlooked the bigger threat posed by disaster capitalism. To counter such problems and threats, we will need as many different kinds of minds working together as fast and effectively as possible to predict the catastrophes most likely to happen next. We need to pre-empt them, if at all possible, and to prepare for them, should they occur.

All of this suggests that the anti-shock doctrine offers not only a whole new leadership role for the professional community, one that can benefit millions of people and save billions of dollars in damage, but also a whole new way of thinking about practice in creating work that no one might commission by revealing what lies in wait for us all. It may come as a shock to those few who have profited from it, but the shock doctrine may end up being just the thing the rest of us needed to shock us into action.

6

Redefining Success

What kind of action do we need to take? The ecology of ecosystems can help us answer that question, since human civilization, for all of its apparent difference from the natural world around it, remains an ecosystem nevertheless, and the same principles apply. Healthy ecosystems comprise relatively homogenous and semi-autonomous units that landscape ecologists call a "patch." Ecosystems exist as a mosaic of diverse patches within a "matrix" of background elements of soil, water, and the atmosphere, the heat and light from the sun, and the living organisms that underpin the entire ecosystem.[1]

The human equivalent of these elements would include small communities of people—families, tribes, settlements, villages—that once existed as relatively homogenous and semi-autonomous patches within the matrix of nature—the plants and animals upon which humans depended on for survival. Healthy human ecosystems would, in turn, have the same characteristic as the non-human kind. No one settlement or group would become so large or so dominant that it would destroy the patchwork-like quality of the whole or overpower the underlying matrix of elements that support human populations: the soil quality needed to sustain farming, for example, or the diversity of living organisms needed to maintain a healthy predator–prey cycle among animals.

Humans managed to live this way for thousands of years, and we know, as a species, how to do this. Such an existence, of course, may

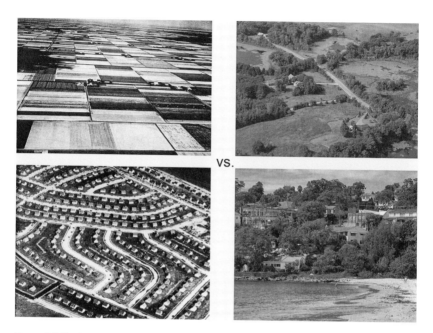

Figure 6.1 Healthy human ecosystems, like those in nature, include a diversity of patches, something rarely recognized in uniformly applied public policies. We need to find a way, instead, to balance equity and fairness with policies that encourage diversity and experimentation at a local level.

seem primitive to us, who have become accustomed to modern life, but that perception says more about our own presumptiveness than it does about the way in which our ancestors once lived. The ability to meet all of their needs with such simple means, based on what they had in their immediate environment, and to accommodate whole populations while leaving behind almost no waste and hardly a trace of their occupation—such characteristics of "primitive" people shows just how smart, skilled, and sophisticated they were and still are in isolated settlements around the world. We have much to learn from those who preceded us and who predate the pretension that underlies our ideas of progress.

A key aspect of that learning comes in understanding earlier ideas of connectedness, in contrast to our own. Human societies have never had greater connectivity than we do now, with bits of information streaming around the world electronically almost instantaneously, with airplanes full of bodies flying around the world almost constantly, and with accumulations of toxins flowing through the air and water almost continuously. We have made Marshall McLuhan's metaphor of the global village a reality, for good and bad.[2] While the hyper-connectivity of our global human population has provided opportunities for many people seeking a better life and has increased our understanding of the value and virtue of diverse cultures and peoples, it has also turned the entire planet into one single, human-dominated patch, one that has overwhelmed the matrix of soil, water, and atmosphere that we depend on, along with all the other species with whom we share the planet.

This has stemmed from an assumption that the faster we can connect and the farther our connections, the better off we will be. Most of the conveyance technologies we have developed over the last century or so—from high-speed trains and planes to high-speed satellite and fiber-optic communications—have sought to compress the time of moving bodies and bits and to overcome the spatial separation that once divided human populations into myriad patches. The quantity of our connections—how many we can have in how short an amount of time—has trumped other forms of connectivity. Increasing numbers of people have "friends" on Facebook and participate in virtual communities of various sorts, but that has paralleled the growing isolation of people in their physical locations, reducing their participation in volunteer or community activities, as Robert Putnam has documented.[3] As a result, people may feel connected to others, but our actual connectedness has a one-dimensional and fracture-critical aspect to it. With a power blackout, a computer problem, or network congestion, the digital connection disappears and the virtual community collapses. Also, technology tends to divide the globe into those who have access to it and those who do not, exacerbating the economic inequities that have become increasingly pronounced in recent decades.

The dilemma here seems endemic to human beings as we develop new technologies. We seem unable to balance the new with the old

The Global Digital Divide

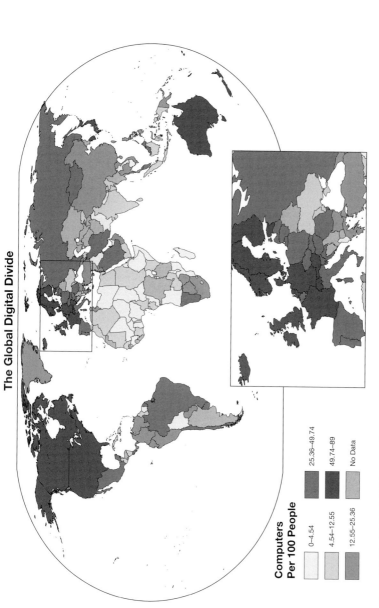

Computers
Per 100 People

0–4.54	25.36–49.74
4.54–12.55	49.74–89
12.55–25.36	No Data

Figure 6.2 The "digital divide" between the northern and southern hemispheres has made it harder for developing nations to participate in the global economy and climb out of poverty.

to maintain multiple ways of doing things. Look at an earlier technology of connectivity: the automobile. When first developed, it
promised to connect people over longer distances and to connect
them to nature in ways sometimes difficult to do before. The early
manufacturers of automobiles marketed them this way, showing
people able to drive to a distant farm, or take a weekend drive for a
picnic in the country or even for a holiday trip to camp in nature.
Had cars remained as such, complementing the other means of
moving around—trains, trolleys, walking, and bicycle riding, to name
just a few—the new technology would have enhanced people's lives
without the downsides of our current dependence on automobiles.
The car would have been a technological "patch" in a matrix of
multiple modes of transportation rather than a "weed" technology
that has marginalized most other means of transportation.

Nor do we seem able to retain diversity within each technological
patch. The early automobile industry contained companies that
offered electric and steam-powered cars as well as those with
gasoline engines.[4] Advertisements promoted electric cars as ideal for
quick trips around town, since they did not have the power of gas
cars or their capability for long-distance driving, but electrics had
other advantages: simple, easily repaired engines; quiet, easily
maneuverable operation; and, of course, no exhaust or emissions.
Steam cars rivaled the power and distance traveled of gas ones, with
a readily available fuel (water) and a harmless emission (water vapor),
making them the ideal everyman's car. Gasoline automobiles, in
contrast, had the most complicated engines, dirtiest operation, and
most expensive fuel, but they also had something the competitors
didn't: Henry Ford and John D. Rockefeller, who, together with the
owners of a few other gas-car companies, ensured that gasoline
automobiles would prevail.

Imagine the world now, had all three types of cars remained in
development and production: fewer greenhouse gases from the
burning of fossil fuel, less dependence on sometimes hostile countries for their oil, less pressure to "drill baby drill" in deep-sea
locations. The desire to corner markets and to eradicate competitors

may constitute an understandable human urge, but this ends up making an entire industry—in this case, the automobile industry— into a single, global patch. In the current economic ecosystem, such patches no longer have any relationship to a particular place, as they do in the rest of the natural world and as they did for human communities prior to the modern era. Instead, the patch becomes any company or technology that can become a "category killer," so dominant that it crowds out all diversity and any real competition.

Contrary to their appearance of unity, consistency, and efficiency, monocultures and monopolies like this have great fragility and little resilience when the context and conditions within which they become dominant dramatically change or quickly disappear. Look at how rapidly the instability of price or availability of oil has caused the fossil-fuel dependent automobile industry not just to become financially stressed, but also to see major companies like General Motors on the verge of bankruptcy.[5] To protect ourselves from such sudden collapses, we need to design our human-made ecosystems— our technologies, economies, and communities—in ways that mimic the characteristics of healthy natural ecosystems, with discrete and semi-autonomous patches of diverse elements.

That will necessitate thinking about the invisible hand of the marketplace as well as the more visible hand of public policy as a way of ensuring diverse opportunities for niche players and as a way of preventing any one entity or technology from becoming too dominant. That may seem like tampering with the free market, but in fact it protects markets from the domination by a few, which stifles competition and, ironically, makes the dominant player in a market liable to catastrophic collapse. Scale matters greatly here. A dominant company, country, or technology, whether at a local, regional, or global scale, endangers us all, and so preventing domination by any one element at every one of those scales becomes essential. Some politicians may see such companies as "too big to fail," but they are also more likely to fail because they are too big.[6]

This may appear to remove the incentive for people to want to strive to develop technologies, improve systems, and grow businesses in our "winner takes all" approach to markets in countries like the United States.[7] This assumes, though, that we can only measure success quantitatively, by how dominant a technology, how extensive a system, or how large a company has become. Instead, we need to develop qualitative measures as the real gage of our success. How much has a technology improved our lives and the health of the environments in which we live? How much has a system enhanced the resiliency and strength of the other systems that it complements? And how much has a company created a higher quality of life for its workers, its customers, and everyone else affected by its activities?

Such questions may seem naive to those cynics who take a fundamentalist approach to capitalism. They are, though, the kinds of questions we have to ask if we are to thrive in a much different world than the one we have just left behind. The answers to them will come once we recognize that we remain absolutely interconnected with all other beings—other humans, future generations, and other species—so that we harm ourselves every time we harm any of these others. We can design a world that does no harm, to borrow medicine's Hippocratic oath. Nature offers examples of this all around us: nothing in nature goes to waste and everything becomes food for something else.[8] That humans remain the only species that generates waste that no one else can use, as well as the only species that has instigated the extinction of large numbers of other species and altered the very balance of the global ecosystem, shows how bad a job we have done designing our world. Our brute-force way of relating to nature and to each other cannot last, and the more we force our way forward to the detriment of others, the more we will force our own demise. That, in the end, remains the main message of the disaster-laden world we now inhabit. We will either quickly and willingly change our ways, or we will find ourselves forced to do so via the disasters we have brought upon ourselves.

PART II

How Fracture-Critical Design Affects Our Lives

7

Fracture-Critical Species

We have designed and built so many fracture-critical systems over the last century that it makes it hard to know which to tackle first. The following sections will discuss several of these systemic failures in greater depth and offer alternatives to them that may help us avert the worst of the disasters that lie ahead and enable us to recover from catastrophes in such a way that we don't just repeat the errors that have caused the problems to begin with. We need to start with the biggest threat of all, the one that, if we don't come to grips with it soon, will make all the other looming disasters irrelevant: the exponential increase in human population over the last sixty years, which could threaten the very survivability of our species.

That may sound hyperbolic, so accustomed have we become to thinking of our species as being at the top of the pyramid of life, with the mental capacity, social complexity, and technological capability to deal with almost anything that might threaten our existence. And obviously we have succeeded at that in the past. Indeed, scientists now talk about the current era in the planet's history as the "anthropocene," a word coined in 2000 by atmospheric chemist Paul Jozef Crutzen to capture the dominance of the human species over almost all aspects of life on earth.[1] Some date the beginning of the anthropocene to the rise of agricultural societies and others to the industrial revolution, but it seems indisputable that humans now hold the fate of most other species—as well as our own—in our hands.

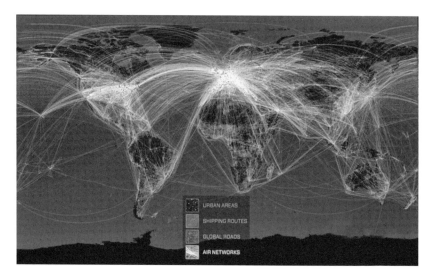

Figure 7.1 Our "anthropocene" world has become so dominated by human activity that no part of the globe remains unaffected by us. That has made us responsible for the health of the planet, for with it goes the health of our species and our ability to survive.

Given that power, why should we feel threatened? If we are in control, why can't we assure our own success, let alone our survivability? Such questions may sound rhetorical, since the answers to them seem obvious, but as environmental historian Jared Diamond has documented we humans have a habit of bringing on our own demise. In his book *Collapse: How Societies Choose to Fail or Succeed*, Diamond shows how human communities in places as disparate as Easter Island, Greenland, and Central America have, in the past, exhausted the very resources people needed in order to survive. The collapse of a human population and community on an island or in a remote corner of the world may constitute a tragedy, but it becomes truly catastrophic at a global scale, since we have no other planet to escape to.[2]

Biologist and science writer Randolph Femmer captures the nature of this threat well in his book *What Every Citizen Should Know About Our Planet*.[3] We tend to think of the collapse of a species as a slow decline in population until it disappears, and so we can easily see our situation, with an exponentially growing human population, as anything but threatened by extinction. But many species face a population collapse following a growth pattern similar to our own. Femmer refers to a study of a reindeer herd on St. Paul Island in Alaska, where the reindeer population, with no predators or other competitors on the island, rose at an exponential rate until it plummeted, with a die-off of 99 percent of the animals. This happened even though most of the island remained uninhabited by reindeer, with ample food and water left.

Femmer makes a couple points worth considering as we contemplate the fracture-critical nature of our own species. The nature of exponential growth encourages us to underestimate a threat to a species. Because exponential growth involves regular increases of something at a fixed percentage, a relatively small quantity can become enormously large very quickly. When it comes to a species and its habitat, such growth in an animal or plant population can make it seem as if ample space and resources remain, just prior to the species running out of what it needs to sustain itself.

Also, we tend to confuse available space with the carrying capacity of an environment. An exponentially growing population, like those reindeer on St. Paul Island, had plenty of physical space, so it might seem odd that the herd experienced a die-off with ample grazing land still available. But the herd outpaced the carrying capacity of the island—the ability of its ecosystem to support that number of one species. While there may remain ample physical space, the waste a species generates, the pollution it causes, the devastation it wreaks on other species, and the imbalances it creates in the ecosystem generally define the capacity of a habitat to support the population.

Those two points—the deceiving nature of exponential growth and the confusion between space and carrying capacity—become particularly relevant as we consider the situation facing our own species. As Femmer observes, the human population has experienced "hyper-exponential" growth. Reaching one billion people globally in 1830, we reached two billion in 1930, one hundred years later; three billion in 1960, thirty years later; four billion in 1975, fifteen years later; five billion in 1987, twelve years later; six billion in 2000, thirteen years later; and seven billion in 2011, eleven years later.[4] Like the reindeer on that Alaska island, we have few predators or competitors on earth and plenty of uninhabited land on our own island in space. But the growth in our numbers has increased even faster than that of the St. Paul Island reindeer herd and we find ourselves pushing up against the limits of the planet's carrying capacity.

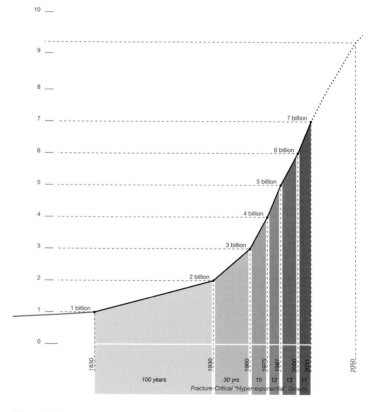

Figure 7.2 World population growth through history. The exponential increase in human population since 1930 makes our own numbers the greatest challenge we face as a species. It will require that we carefully steward finite resources, rapidly develop renewable ones, and intelligently husband other species in order to sustain our own.

Indeed, with the current human ecological footprint larger than the planet itself, we may have already outpaced that capacity. There remain doubters, of course. Julian Simon, a professor of business administration at the University of Maryland, has argued that human ingenuity and technological innovation will enable us to devise ways of supporting our very large human population, and he has plenty of evidence from the nineteenth and twentieth centuries to support his claim.[5] Innovations in food and energy production, for example, have enabled us to accommodate our exponentially growing population, itself the result of improvements in medical technology and public health efforts that have reduced death rates in many parts of the world.

What Simon's appealingly optimistic argument leaves out, though, is the fracture-critical nature of the human population as a result of those innovations. We can feed many more people as a result of the "green revolution" that agronomist Norman Borlaug helped set in motion, but that revolution has also led to a cascading number of other problems—water pollution, soil exhaustion, expensive seed stocks—and to our dependence, as a species, on a relatively few staples—rice, wheat, and maize or corn.[6] The more our species relies on the health of a few plants even as we put more environmental and economic stress on the system, the more vulnerable we become to the failure of a key component and a collapse of the food system. A rapidly spreading disease in just one of those key staples, for example, would lead to a major disruption of the food supply and widespread hunger and starvation as a possible result.

It does not appear, at first, as if the positions of people like Femmer and Simon have any common ground. Those who advocate for population control often see it as a matter of our avoiding the fate of the St. Paul Island reindeer, a die-off that might kill 99 percent or more of the human population, something, of course, that no one wants. And yet those who put their faith in human ingenuity to solve whatever survivability problems our exponentially growing population might encounter also make a legitimate point. We will need as much creativity, persistence, and focus as we can muster if we are to avert the disaster of our own undoing as a species.

These two apparently polar opposite positions, in other words, do not represent mutually exclusive points of view. We cannot keep growing our numbers at such a rate without altering our ecological footprint so that we remain within the carrying capacity of the planet. Those who think that a human population our size can continue to over-consume resources and over-produce waste beyond what the earth can handle simply kid themselves and, ironically, make an anti-innovation argument. The real innovation needed, the real design task we face, involves creating a high-quality life for all people within the limits the planet can sustain. We don't entirely know how to do that yet, but we need to start figuring that out quickly, for we have very little time.

Jared Diamond has estimated that we have about fifty years before we see the effects of the exponential declines in natural habitats, fish populations, biological diversity, and farmable soil; before we reach a ceiling on inexpensive fossil fuels, accessible fresh water, and plant growth per acre; and before we see the effects of exponential increases in toxic chemicals in the air and water, invasive plant species devastating ecosystems, ozone-depleting atmospheric gases, impoverished human populations, and unsustainable levels of consumption.[7] Diamond argues that we need to attend to all of the items on this list if we are to avoid a collapse of civilization, at least as we have known it, although some of the challenges he identifies should worry us more than others. We can live without inexpensive fossil fuels; we cannot live without access to fresh water.

How we innovate, in other words, matters a great deal. Innovation that creates fracture-critical systems that have to work perfectly in order to support large segments of the human population only makes us more vulnerable to catastrophes, not less so. And as we saw with a fracture-critical system like the I-35W Bridge, its sudden failure can occur despite the best efforts of people to prevent it from happening. Allowing our numbers to rise exponentially as we let the ecosystems that support us decline at an equally exponential rate becomes suicidal unless we aggressively change the way in which we inhabit the planet: dramatically reducing the toxins we manufacture, the carbon we emit, the habitat we destroy, the fresh water we use, and the amount and type of food we consume. The alternative — a massive die-off of human beings — is the kind of collapse that we must do absolutely everything we can to avoid.

Re-sizing the Human Footprint

8

How might we go about redesigning our ecological footprint as a species in order avoid this fate? Rarely do design problems come with such stark terms, as literally a life-or-death situation for us all. That doesn't make the challenge, however, any less amenable to the kind of design thinking we would bring to other, less momentous problems. If anything, with humanity's extinction in the balance, the process might go somewhat more smoothly, since it becomes hard to refuse to engage in it or walk away from it, unless we want to commit a kind of collective annihilation. So where might we begin?

The research by the Global Footprint Network offers one starting point. A recent paper by several scholars in the network shows how the per-capita ecological footprint, which measures how much biologically productive land and water it takes to support a person at current levels of consumption, tends in most countries to grow faster than the Human Development Index (HDI) developed by the United Nations as a measure of our progress toward improving the lives of people. "Only five countries (Burundi, Cuba, Cote D'Ivoire, Malawi, and Uruguay)," conclude the authors, "increased their HDI without increasing their Footprint to biocapacity," and "only one country of the 93 surveyed (Cuba) met the two specified minimum requirements for development within a consumption pattern that could be extended globally without entering over-shoot."[1]

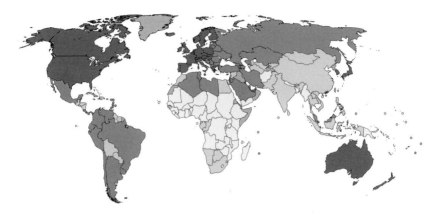

Figure 8.1 We are consuming resources at a faster rate than we are improving the quality of life of people as measured by the Human Development Index (HDI). We need to design a future for ourselves that reverses that relationship, improving our lives while using fewer resources, not more. The darker-toned countries in the above map consume resources faster than the lighter-toned countries, which rank lower on the HDI.

I would be the last to suggest that we adopt Cuba's political culture, with its Castro-led government. But, especially now that Cuba has become more open to the rest of the world, we have a lot we might learn from that country as a possible model for how humanity can lead a relatively high quality of life within the carrying capacity of the planet. Some have mocked the idea of Cuba as a model, unable to separate the sustainable lifestyle of its people from the dictatorial ideology of its government, as if the way people live in that country stems from their lack of political freedom. But, however much we might justifiably criticize the Cuban government, we should not equate sustainable living with repressive politics. We will have no choice but to live more sustainably and so we need to find ways of doing so other than through a totalitarian system.

We don't have to look to Cuba, however. U.S. history also offers us models of how to do this. Only relatively recently has the average American lived way beyond the carrying capacity of the planet, with an amount of consumption that would require over five earths to sustain the human species at that same level. However, throughout most of U.S. history, we, like most of the rest of the world, lived within a sustainable ecological footprint, and we did so with a democratically elected government. As recently as 1975, the average U.S. citizen consumed at a rate only three times the carrying capacity of the earth, obviously still too high, but almost half the level at which we consume now. Likewise the average rate of consumption across the planet, now at about 1.5 earths, stood well within the carrying capacity of the globe in 1975, so we don't need to go back very far to see how we might live in the future in a way that can sustain our exponentially increasing numbers.[2]

Moran et al. suggest one design direction: "Increasing affluence is by no means intrinsically incongruous with the goal of maintaining the health of the biosphere. Transitioning out of fossil fuels, encouraging resource efficient urban infrastructure, and providing support for people who are choosing to have smaller families are three demonstrated steps which can help make development sustainable."[3] Rather than dismiss such recommendations through association with Cuba or claim that any limits on people's consumption habits amounts to a constraint on freedom, we would do well to get on with imagining a high-quality, freedom-loving life that recognizes that we don't have four other earths out there just waiting for us to inhabit. True freedom does not come by doing whatever we want if that threatens to push our species along with many others to extinction. Instead, it comes from living within our means, economically and ecologically, without having the financial or environmental debt we have taken on constantly threatening to crush us.

Living in more compact settlements, where we can meet our needs without having to get into a fossil-fueled automobile, remains one obvious direction we should take. No Cuban-style plot to limit people's freedom, this simply means that we should recognize what our ancestors knew all too well: that humans do better and their environments remain healthier when we can secure more of our needs within walking distance, seeing neighbors, watching over children, and attending to our community in the process. Growing and making what we need mostly locally remains a part of such a life as well. This not only supports the economy of our communities, but also reduces our dependence upon distant producers and other countries for our needs. Self-reliance has stood at the center of how humans have lived over most of our history, and we need to return to that frame of mind, without letting the sometimes extreme ideological debates of the political right and left get in our way.

Not letting anything go to waste remains another obvious step we need to take in order to live within our global footprint. This has to go beyond recycling to include the redesign of what we consume, how we consume it, and where the remains of our consumption go. So much of our current consumption involves packaging designed to transport goods intact over tremendously long distances and products that have obsolescence designed into them, to force us to buy anew even if most of the old product remains useable. That throw-away culture of goods and services has helped propel us way past where we stood even three or four decades ago. We need to rediscover what our grandparents and great-grandparents did as a matter of course: reuse what we can, recycle what we can't, and refrain from buying anything new if there remains a way for us to utilize what the waste stream already contains. Those earlier generations also had the concept of an heirloom, a valued possession handed down through a family, cared for and treasured by those who will eventually pass it on themselves. We have replaced heirlooms with new-and-improved products that have a short lifespan and few qualities we would even want to hand down to our children.

Having fewer children remains a part of this as well. While our ancestors often had larger families because not every child made it to adulthood and because families often needed as many hands as possible to work, especially on a farm, they rarely had more children than they could feed and care for, and we should do the same. Globally, we cannot feed the population we have now without so damaging the biosphere's soil and water that the problem will only get worse for our children and grandchildren. While improvements in agriculture will help us address this problem, we will have no choice but to accept limits on the number of children we have and accept penalties for having more than our replacement.

So whether we look to Cuba now or to the North America that our great grandparents handed down to us, the answer looks much the same. We will all have to start living in much more compact mixed-use settlements, in much more modest living quarters, with much more of our goods and services provided locally, and with whole industries focused on the recycling, reuse, or repurposing of almost everything. This will mean a transition for many who live too far out, in too large a house, dependent on too much driving in order to get almost everything they need, but our economy, especially after the Great Recession, has already started to take care of that, since the market for such a way of living has begun to shrink rapidly. Some six decades after building suburbia, we will begin to see much of it bulldozed and the rest of it densified, with more buildings filling in all the space we once wasted.[4] And after a century or so of dismissing what our ancestors knew, we will begin to see our descendants living within their ecological footprint once again, as they look back on the twentieth-century generations and wonder what on earth were we thinking.

9

Fracture-Critical Population

One of greatest threats to us may be not in what we see or in the things we can command, but in what remains invisible and often beyond our control: viruses. Rapidly rising human populations living in increasingly unsanitary conditions combined with rapid transcontinental air travel have made a catastrophic viral pandemic more likely than ever before, affecting daily life and the global economy in profound ways. And we have only begun to assess the impact this will have on our daily lives. This was explored in an exhibition at the Storefront for Art and Architecture in New York entitled "Landscapes of Quarantine." Curated by Geoff Manaugh of BLDGBLOG and Nicola Twilley of Edible Geography, the exhibition brought together eighteen architects, artists, and designers whose work deals with quarantine in some way.[1] While many places of quarantine exist, for obvious reasons in isolated places, some do occur in urban settings, such as the quarantine islands that once existed near cities such as Venice and New York. As the exhibition's curators note, "The practice of quarantine extends far beyond questions of epidemic control and pest-containment strategies to touch on issues of urban planning, geopolitics, international trade, ethics, immigration, and more."[2]

The curators also recognize the long history of our trying to control viral epidemics: "The practice dates back at least to the arrival of the Black Death in medieval Venice, if not to Christ's 40 days in the desert."[3] But a turning point in the history of epidemics occurred in 1854, when Dr. John Snow traced a cholera outbreak in London to contaminated water in a well on Broad Street, marking the beginning of the modern profession of public health.[4] Snow's discovery not only dispelled the then-common "miasma" theory of disease, which attributed illness to "bad air," but also made illness a geographical issue, connecting epidemics to particular causes in specific places. All of a sudden urban design and infrastructure mattered both in the conveyance of disease and in its prevention.

That had a tremendous effect on architecture, engineering, and urban design. In New York City later in the nineteenth century, cholera and malaria outbreaks led to building and zoning codes that controlled overcrowding, mandated more sanitary conditions, and propelled infrastructure investments that have influenced urban systems and services to this day. Indeed, those codes have served us so well over the last century that we have possibly become too complacent about the new public health threats that have arisen in cities around the world. As Manaugh and Twilley write, "quarantine has reemerged as an issue of urgency and importance in today's era of globalization, antibiotic resistance, emerging diseases, pandemic flu, and bio-terrorism."[5]

That has become particularly urgent given the speed with which we can now transport a viral infection around the globe via air travel. Despite the vast geographical distances among us, the entire human population remains almost equally exposed to pandemic disease, and we all need to take this threat seriously and design accordingly. That needs saying since the relative mildness of the 2009 H1N1 influenza outbreak might lead many to dismiss the severity of the threat. Thousands of people did die as a result of H1N1—nearly 5,000 globally according to the World Health Organization—but not enough to prompt a dramatic increase in preventative measures.[6] However, we may not be so lucky the next time. Viral infections like Ebola hemorrhagic fever can kill quickly and no vaccine yet exists to fight them.[7] And North Americans have only to look at our own history for evidence of how deadly a viral infection can be, given the

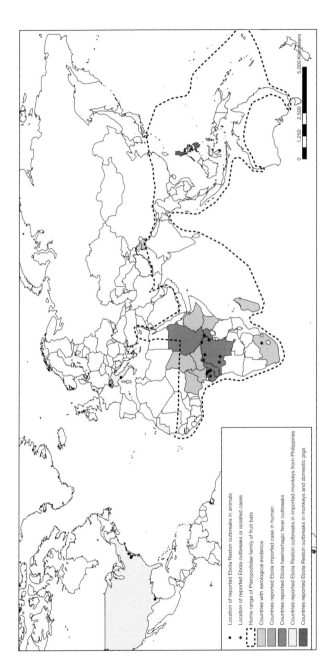

Figure 9.1 Geographic distribution of Ebola haemorrhagic fever outbreaks and fruit bats of Pteropodidae Family. We have all benefited from high-speed, global air travel, but with that convenience has come one of the greatest threats to our existence as a species: the ability to transmit virulent disease, for which no vaccine exists, rapidly through the human population.

Location of reported Ebola Reston outbreaks in animals

Location of reported Ebola outbreaks or isolated cases

Home range of Pteropodidae family of fruit bats

Countries with serological evidence

Countries reported Ebola imported case in human

Countries reported Ebola haemorrhagic fever outbreaks

Countries reported Ebola Reston outbreaks in imported monkeys from Philippines

Countries reported Ebola Reston outbreaks in monkeys and domestic pigs

0   1,250   2,500   5,000 Kilometers

devastation of the native populations in the wake of European arrival on the continent.

This gives new meaning to Marshall McLuhan's idea of the "global village." He saw electronic media making the globe more village-like in the sense that we would have the instant communication and constant connectedness worldwide that people used to have in small communities.[8] What McLuhan didn't see is that the global village, when it becomes literally true through high-speed trade and travel, can also become a threat to the health of every person in it, by connecting us into a single community of disease against which many of us may have little or no immunity. The media may, indeed, hold the key here. The need to protect ourselves against pandemics and slow the possible transmission of disease until we can immunize ourselves against it may, in turn, require that we depend ever more on the moving of bits of information rather than of human bodies or boxes of goods around the world, limiting travel and trade even though we have the means to do so faster and more efficiently than ever.

That prospect will surely raise all sorts of objections, since it goes against the idea of physical freedom and the faith in technological progress that have come to characterize modern life. Might a globe of more physically isolated communities return us to a more-or-less primitive existence, haunted by the tribal conflicts, ethnic prejudices, and fear of strangers that have characterized human communities in the past? And might barriers to travel impose too great a restriction on our ability to experience other places and other cultures and too great a constraint on the ability of individuals to reach their greatest potential beyond the bounds of the communities in which they were born?

These are precisely the questions we need to raise and address as we go forward, since it makes no sense to protect our physical health if political repression or social oppression comes as a result. Virally resistant cities should be healthier places in all aspects of our lives, not virtual prisons for people. To help prevent the latter from happening, we might take advantage of another type of virus: the cultural virus that biologist Richard Dawkins first called a "meme" in his book *The Selfish Gene*. Memes constitute compelling ideas that can replicate in the minds of other people, increasing the intellectual diversity of a community, while also "killing off" an existing concept or an unexamined assumption of a culture.[9]

One of the challenges we have in fighting actual viruses is that we cannot see them, and so we downplay their importance: we find it easier to picture a bomb-wielding anarchist than we do a bio-terrorist, even though the latter may pose a much greater threat to us all. For that reason, it becomes especially important to make viruses more visible and thus more viable as something we need to pay attention to, which is a role that the meme of "viral cities" might play. The physical transformation of our cities and communities in an effort to protect us from pandemics has not only the benefit of public health, but also the advantage of turning this into an issue real to many people, making it immediate and tangible in ways that no amount of public pronouncements ever could.

That takes us to the heart of a debate among those who study memes, "memeticists" as cognitive scientist Douglas Hofstadter first called them.[10] Memetic "internalists" focus on the cognitive aspects of ideas, paying relatively little attention to the physical environ-ments that give rise to ideas, while the "externalists" argue that physical contexts matter and that they can both encourage and reflect changes in our thinking. From my reading of this literature, the internalists appear to have won the debate, with neuroscience and cognitive psychology dominating the field.

However, when it comes to transferring the "meme" of biological viruses as the primary shaper of human life in the twenty-first century, the externalists may have the edge. It may be that the phy-sical environment, despite all of the electronic means now available to us to discover and transfer ideas, may once again become funda-mental to our understanding of and our acting upon the real viral threat. Only through changes in our actual behavior—in our travel expectations, work habits, living patterns, social customs, and self-conceptions—will we be able to slow a pandemic enough to develop a vaccine for it and immunity against it.

That has put us in a race of sorts as to which virus embeds itself in the human population first. Will it be the conceptual meme of "viral cities" that gets us to rethink our daily activities and our responsibilities to others as the best way to protect ourselves? Or will it be the virulent gene in some actual virus for which we have no cure, that arrives by stealth via an infected airline passenger and that spreads rapidly through the population faster than we can react? Let us hope it is the former and not the latter, although the history of cities suggests otherwise. It seems that people rarely act against an invisible threat until they have suffered the consequences of ignoring it, as happened in Venice in the fourteenth century or London in the nineteenth century. Maybe this time it will be different. If we start to take the current threat seriously and not dismiss it as too remote a possibility to worry about, we may beat the odds and avoid the worst of what the pandemics headed our way have to offer. Place your bets.

10

Protective Design

What does it mean to design with viruses in mind? We might take some cues from how we protect ourselves from viruses in the digital environment. A computer virus can cripple the hardware and subvert its software, preventing us from working or communicating. To avoid this, we have at least three options:

1 We can go to the source of the virus and try to stop its spread.
2 We can try to erect digital firewalls and install virus-detection software to prevent its arrival.
3 We can try to prevent infection by distancing ourselves from it and not opening attachments.[1]

While such efforts rarely provide complete protection, they can go a long way to reducing the likelihood of a viral attack on computers. And they suggest ways in which we might design our cities in order to respond to actual viruses let loose in our population.

The first line of defense involves addressing the source of a viral pandemic. While viruses can mutate and spread almost anywhere, certain environments make it more likely to happen. The rapid growth of overcrowded cities and informal settlements in impoverished parts of the world has increased the incidence of unsanitary living conditions that can generate and spread deadly zoonoses: diseases that transfer from animals to humans when both live in close proximity to each other. With global slums now accommodating over one billion people, a number expected to double over the next three decades, the chance of an outbreak of zoonotic disease has also gone up rapidly.[2]

Nor can we assume that the development and spread of such disease will always be unintentional. The combination of disease-ridden slums with the sense of hopelessness that comes from living in such conditions has also made infectious disease a possible weapon of bio-terrorists. As Mike Davis writes in *Planet of Slums*, "the 'feral, failed cities' of the Third World—especially their slum outskirts—will be the distinctive battle space of the twenty-first century. Pentagon doctrine is being reshaped accordingly to support a low-intensity world war of unlimited duration against criminalized segments of the urban poor. This is the true 'clash of civilizations'."[3]

Whether done for humanitarian, personal health, or anti-terrorism reasons, addressing the living conditions that give rise to such outbreaks has become an urgent matter. Helping the billion people who live in inadequate shelter and unsanitary conditions may seem like an overwhelming task, but it may also be the wisest investment we can make. It is a very cost-effective investment as well. The Centers for Disease Control and Prevention estimate that the economic impact of a pandemic would be between $71 billion and $166 billion, excluding the cost of disruptions to commerce and society, which would likely increase the cost considerably.[4] Compare that cost to the $16 billion lent for shelter improvement by the World Bank in ninety countries over the last thirty-four years, and it seems evident that the investments made in addressing the likely source of pandemic disease has not come close to matching the risk involved.[5]

Even if we commit much more money to improving the living conditions of the globe's slum-dwellers, as we should, it will remain a long-term goal almost out of necessity. The scale of the needs and the diversity of conditions people face will limit the speed with which significant physical improvements can occur. Which leads to the second strategy: building firewalls and detection methods to prevent viruses from spreading. The place to start is at international airports.[6] Although no one intended this, airline travel has become the most efficient means of transferring disease ever invented in human history, able to send a virus to which we have no defense around the world in a matter of hours and to infect millions of people before we even know what has happened.

Research done in the wake of the H1N1 pandemic has found a high correlation between the disease's transmission and airline flights from Mexico in March and April, 2009.[7] As the authors of the study state, "international air travelers departing from Mexico were unknowingly transporting a novel influenza A (H1N1) virus to cities around the world." Although many people may associate contagious diseases with isolated or impoverished parts of the world, viruses become pandemic first in the most economically active and globally connected cities, which tend to have the busiest airports and the most flights to and from the greatest number of other places.

Cities have a long history of fighting disease at their ports and other points of entry. After medieval Venice suffered a series of epidemics, the government in the fourteenth and fifteenth centuries quarantined sailors and their cargo on a separate island for forty days prior to entering the city to ensure that they did not bring disease with them.[8] New York City did something similar with passengers arriving at its port in the nineteenth and early twentieth centuries, quarantining them on Hoffman and Swinburne islands to prevent the spread of illness.[9] And during the 1918 pandemic in the United States some communities required health certificates from visitors before allowing them to enter.[10]

In the age of global airline travel, efforts to slow the spread of disease through the quarantine of arriving passengers long enough to determine their state of health seems inconceivable. But it has already begun to happen, as many experienced during the H1N1 outbreak. The U.S. government warned passengers that "their travel may be delayed" and that they might have to "pass through a scanning device that checks your temperature" and "be quarantined for a period of time if a passenger on your flight is found to have symptoms of H1N1 flu."[11]

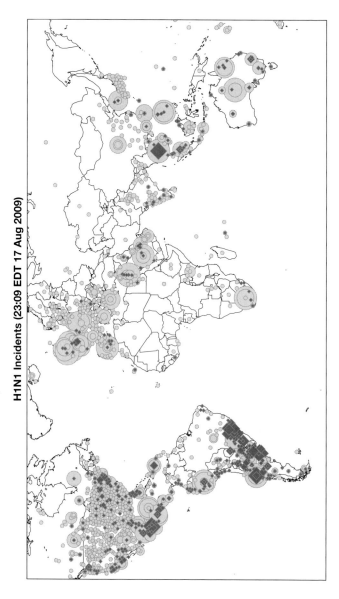

H1N1 Incidents (23:09 EDT 17 Aug 2009)

Figure 10.1 The wealthiest and most-traveled people remain the most exposed to viral disease because of their use of and proximity to airports, which counters the assumption that the rich will be able insulate themselves from a pandemic. Better to address the conditions that cause viral outbreaks rather than try to avoid them.

The risk of disease transmission may eventually change not only the way we travel, but also the way in which we work and relate to each other globally. The old adage of "think globally, act locally" may well come literally true as mobile video technology has now developed to the point where we can communicate seamlessly in real time with anyone anywhere in the world, without having to leave home. Also, as we become increasingly aware of the environmental damage caused by air travel and as the cost of such travel will likely increase with rising fuel prices, the need to move our bodies physically around the world may come to seem irresponsible and wasteful. We all may become less physically connected, even as we become more so electronically.

As we have learned in the digital environment, we can often avoid a computer virus by not opening unfamiliar attachments that may infect our machine. The equivalent of that in the physical environment involves what public health physicians call "social distancing." "In the event of a serious pandemic," write Shannon Brownlee and Jeanne Lenzer in *The Atlantic*, "'social distancing' (voluntary quarantines, school closings, and even enforcement of mandatory quarantines to keep infected people in their homes) . . . will require . . . widespread buy-in from the public. Yet little discussion has appeared in the press to help people understand the measures they can take to best protect themselves."[12]

The physical and social implications of this are considerable. Social distancing can take extreme and even inhuman form, as Daniel Defoe recounted in his novel *A Journal of the Plague Year*, when officials locked in everyone in a household if one person showed signs of the plague during the epidemic of 1665.[13] And as we saw during the SARS outbreak in Asia, people do respond to pandemics in ways that alter their behavior in and use of public space: wearing masks, avoiding contact, shunning strangers, staying indoors, and even fleeing cities.[14]

Pandemics can have unintended benefits, as happened when Isaac Newton made some of his key discoveries regarding gravity, motion, and calculus during the eighteen months he spent in relative isolation in his family home in rural Woolsthorpe when Cambridge University closed because of the plague.[15] But most people will need more support to remain productive in the midst of the social distancing that an outbreak of infectious disease will demand. Telecommuting offers one option. With nearly one-quarter of the American workforce regularly doing some part of their job from home and 62 percent wishing they could do so, the ability to keep working while digitally connected provides a way of mixing productivity and social distancing.[16]

With telecommuting comes the need for more mixed-use communities that can provide a range of services to people working as well as living in each neighborhood. This may seem counter to the need for social distancing in the face of pandemics, but it raises, instead, a reality of urban life often forgotten in the modern world: before the era of global travel, most humans lived in viral communities with those who shared exposure and immunity to the same diseases. That made the provision of most human needs within a relatively small geographic area a necessity, a way of limiting our interactions mainly to those with whom we had diseases in common. It also made membership in a community not just a social and economic benefit, but literally a matter of life and death, since traveling too far away from one's own viral community made a person both a threat to others and vulnerable to infection by others.

The prospect of pandemic, in other words, requires that we rethink the current division between those who envision a high-tech future of global connectedness and those who, in contrast, call for a return to traditional, small-scale, mixed-use settlements. In reality, we need aspects of both in a future increasingly threatened by exotic diseases for which we either have no natural immunity or no pharmacological protection.[17] The digital environment will enable us to be globally connected and the provision of goods and services locally will let us meet our daily needs while remaining physically and socially distant from those who do not share our same viral community.

There is also much we can do within communities and in individual buildings to protect people from the spread of viral infection. That might include rethinking the smallest details of daily life, such as the innocent but potentially hazardous gestures of shaking hands or passing paper between two people. And it may involve our paying more attention to those elements of buildings — door knobs, light switches, restroom faucets, and the like — that provide the greatest potential for transmitting disease. Here, too, both the old and the new have much to offer. Hand shaking, for example, used to be a sign of solidarity among people who shared the same viral community, which we might do well to remember when we next greet strangers. At the same time, motion detection and remote sensing technology — now mainly viewed as a convenience — may become a necessity as we seek ways of operating the designed environment without having to come in physical contact with it. We may soon all be living in a "hands-off" world.

11

Fracture-Critical Economy

Finding ways of making the human population more resilient in the face of sudden, unexpected and potentially devastating threats such as a global pandemic, while improving the quality of life of the world's poor without dramatically decreasing the living standards of the rest, remains one of the great tasks before us. We might start by focusing on the quality of life, rather than on, as we so often do now, its quantities, which will demand that we face up to the fracture-critical nature of the current global economy we have created. We have already had a taste of its fracture-critical character with the sudden and catastrophic collapse of much of the global investment banking system in 2008. The Great Recession that this triggered, as many have observed, represented more than just a cyclical economic downturn; it reset the global economy.[1] We know that many of the old practices—the unsustainable amounts of debt on the part of the government, consumers, and lenders, for example, or the highly leveraged nature of investments in high-risk assets—cannot continue. The exact nature and magnitude of this "new normal," however, remains less than clear.

Consider the U.S. government debt, which remains on a course of exponential growth. As recently as 2000, the national debt stood at $6 trillion; ten years later, it stood at $13.6 trillion, with the U.S. Treasury Department expecting it to rise to $19.6 trillion by 2015, more than a threefold increase in just fifteen years.[2] U.S. consumers and banks have shared in this dramatic rise, with consumer debt increasing threefold since 1982.[3] Meanwhile, personal savings rates among Americans hit an all-time low, with a historic 6.9 percent drop in consumers' discretionary spending after 2007.[4] That latter statistic shows what a collapse from a fracture-critical debt-supported economic system looks like: the fall happens suddenly and precipitously, in a cascading fashion, with systemic failure across the board. The U.S. government and its citizens seem like an alcoholic after a binge, with a huge hangover and yet without the will to stop the drinking

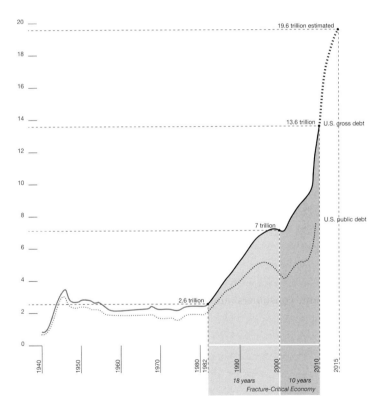

Figure 11.1 Our economic system works a lot like any ecosystem: if we continually stress the system by adding debt beyond our ability to handle it, we will eventually bring the system down, as happened with the global banking collapse in 2008.

or the willingness to see that unless it does, the binges and busts will only get worse in the future.

Nor is the U.S. government or the American public by any means alone in this behavior; many banks have served as the supplier of this debt addiction, and become dramatically overleveraged with debt of their own. Indeed, the catastrophic fall of the Wall Street banks, which triggered the global economic downturn, demonstrated how fast a fracture-critical system, badly designed and poorly regulated, can come crashing down without warning. Part of the blame for this rests with the greed of the bankers and the lethargy of the regulators involved, but part of it also lies with the system itself and the products that it created.[5] In many ways, the fall of the investment banks had the same characteristics of the collapse of the I-35W Bridge. Just as the failure of one set of gusset plates brought that entire bridge down, so too did the failure of a few investment banks — the bankruptcy of Lehman Brothers and the near collapses of Bear Stearns and Merrill Lynch — lead to the fall of the entire system.[6] The cracks that opened up in those institutions set off a chain-reaction collapse of the credit and stock markets around the world, bringing on, as we know, a recession nearly as catastrophic as the worldwide depression of the 1930s.

And just as the highway crews piled on extra weight while resurfacing the I-35W roadway before the bridge went down, so too did the markets pile huge amounts of debt onto the financial system, overloading banks to the point of collapse. An odd aspect of fracture-critical systems lies in our seeming compulsion to stress them until they fail. You might think that if we have designed a system with no redundancy and with a structure that cannot handle any additional loading that we would take care not to overstress it. But like civil engineers in a laboratory, piling weight on a structure with the goal of determining the point at which it will collapse, we have conducted a real-time experiment with the global economy, affecting almost every person on the planet. And we have let a relatively few invest-ment bankers play engineer and see how far they could go before the whole thing came crashing down. The actions of these banks may have fit within the law, but the irresponsibility of their actions remains absolutely astonishing.

Most fracture-critical failures, however, require accomplices. Just as government inspectors and consultants did not catch the problem of deflecting gusset plates on the I-35W Bridge or understand the risk involved in not reinforcing them before they failed, government regulators and independent auditors did not provide enough oversight or have adequate understanding of what a loss of confidence in mortgage-backed securities in one part of the financial system could have on the rest.[7] The bankers seemed to treat some regulators like the lab assistants who would do what they were told, willing to go along and look the other way when the debt load got too great and the investment structure looked like it might topple.

Once we see the collapse of our fracture-critical financial system as an "adaptive cycle," we can begin to see what we will need to do in order to prevent this from happening again: making our global banking system less connected, less efficient, and more resilient as a result. As William Dudley, the president and CEO of the Federal Reserve Bank of New York puts it, we need to take "steps to strengthen the resolution regime and the core financial market infrastructure to ensure that when a large complex financial firm fails, the failure doesn't threaten to bring down the entire financial system."[8] Like making a bridge more resistant to collapse, this might involve creating a financial structure with more discrete, disconnected parts, with strong divisions among them so that even if one aspect of the system fails, the rest will not go down. A redesigned financial system might also need to have more redundant parts, with more checks and balances to ensure that even if someone makes an error of judgment or even a conscious effort to subvert the system, inspectors would catch it before it could lead the entire structure to fail. Finally, a more resilient system might have a slower speed and lower efficiency than the fracture-critical one that preceded it. Transactions might have delays built into them, allowing for extra time and added review in order to ensure that the movement of funds was intentional and not improper. Indeed, the very idea of a globally integrated financial system might itself disappear, as nations hurt by the previous collapse over which they had almost no control set up their own review procedures and regulatory policies to make sure that a worldwide meltdown would not so adversely affect them in the future.

The global scope of the financial meltdown highlights the importance of spotting these potential failures before they occur. It was bad enough for over 150 people to die or be injured as a result of the I-35W Bridge's failure. Seeing the financial losses and negative impact on the lives of millions of people around the world as a result of the financial collapse, leading to a rapid slowdown in the global economy and the bankruptcy of many businesses and individuals, should lead us to make the identification of fracture-critical systems one of our top priorities. Even if we cannot prevent systems in an adaptive cycle from ever collapsing back to a state of greater resiliency, we can prepare people and lessen the blow, especially to those who are most vulnerable.

Rethinking Work

12

Any such change, of course, raises the perennial question over who will win and who will lose in the transition. And it seems, for now at least in the United States, that almost every regulatory reform faces the charge that it would be a "job killer."[1] Of course, those who chant this mantra usually have the most invested in the ways things are and, not wanting to risk change, seek to attract others to their defense by threatening the loss of jobs. And, with the economic disturbances or downturns that often accompany a major economic transition, many people resist change for fear of losing their jobs, leading to the paradoxical situation, as cultural critic Thomas Frank has observed, of "a manipulative ruling class . . . exploit[ing] an impoverished people while simultaneously fostering in them a culture of victimization that steers this people's fury back . . . toward a shadowy, cosmopolitan Other."[2] It's harder, it seems, to let go of what we do know, however much it goes against our long-term interests, than to embrace what we don't, regardless of how much good it would do.

The paradox here is that, while some people want to hold on to the old economy in hopes of not losing their jobs, that old economy has also been very good at shedding jobs in the name of efficiency, replacing people with machines or sending jobs overseas to lower-cost countries.[3] Why hold onto something that eliminates jobs in hopes of protecting jobs? As President Obama wisely observed in a speech at Georgetown University:

We can't go back to that kind of economy. That's not where the jobs are. The jobs of the twenty-first century are in areas like clean energy and technology, advanced manufacturing, new infrastructure. That kind of economy requires us to consume less and produce more; to import less and export more. Instead of sending jobs overseas, we need to send more products overseas that are made by American workers and American business. And we need to train our workers for those jobs with new skills and a world-class education.[4]

That process is already well underway. As anyone following the careers of recent U.S. college graduates knows, the youth of today seem especially skilled at starting new ventures, sometimes right out of school, frequently socially or environmentally beneficial, and often either very hands-on and local in their focus or extremely virtual and global in their reach.[5] They have begun to re-imagine what constitutes work in the process. In Western culture, we tend to conflate jobs with work, so much so that when people lose jobs, we say that they are out of work. It may be in the future, however, that losing a job means having the time to do work that might be more meaningful, satisfying, and even more needed.

As philosopher Hannah Arendt reminds us in her writing about the human condition, jobs and the labor that we do as part of them constitute a necessary part of life in that they enable us to meet our biological needs for food, clothing, shelter, and the like, but rather than minimize this labor to the point where it meets our minimal needs, we have let it take over our lives in pursuit of material abundance.[6] This has led some people to become not "workaholics" so much as "job-aholics," laboring so much that they become slaves to their jobs, even as many other people who have lost their jobs become outcasts in a society that values people according to the labor they do. Instead, as Arendt argued, what makes us most human is our work, what we do to create "permanence, stability, and durability" in the world.[7] While others can take our jobs away from us, no one can take away the work we have to do, the work that means the most to us and that benefits others the most.

Such sentiments may sound overly idealistic in this time of high unemployment, but they also have real practicality since, as economist Jeremy Rifkin has argued, high unemployment will only get worse as the current economy shifts from large numbers of wage-paying jobs to a much smaller number of high-skill, knowledge-based jobs aided by automation and computer technology.[8] He observes:

> In the past seven years alone, 14% of all the manufacturing jobs in the world have disappeared, as more and more human labor has been replaced with intelligent, automated technology. Similar technology displacement is occurring in the white collar and service industries . . . Redefining the role of the individual in a near workerless society is likely to be the most pressing issue in the decades to come . . . Greater reliance will need to be placed on creating new employment opportunities in the emerging "third sector", or civil society.[9]

Rifkin called his best-known book *The End of Work*, although he might have called it instead something like *The End of Jobs and the Rediscovery of Work*, since the employment in the third sector that he calls for entails exactly that: helping people have greater financial resilience in the face of a sometimes rapacious global system, while offering a greater degree of protection from the layoffs that will continue to plague jobholders as we make the transition from the old economy to the new one.

What might such a world based on fulfilling work rather than laborious jobs look like? William Morris's utopian novel *News From Nowhere* offers an intriguing answer to such a question. He envisioned a future in which there existed "the absence of artificial coercion, and the freedom for every man to do what he can do best, joined to the knowledge of what productions of labor we really want."[10] People, in other words, would do what they seemed most interested in and best suited to do. "All work," wrote Morris, should be "pleasurable . . . because of the hope of gain in honor and wealth with which the work is done . . . and lastly (and most of our work is of this kind) because there is conscious sensuous pleasure in the work itself; it is done, that is, by artists."[11]

This sounds utopian, of course, and, like all utopias, it immediately brings practical questions to mind, such as who will do the unpleasant jobs that need doing and how would people have the means to buy even the necessities of life if everyone did what they wanted? Morris argued for a socialist society that would collectively take care of necessities and people's basic needs, but his view of a work-oriented, as opposed to a jobs-oriented, world does not require a socialist or communist political system in order to succeed. Morris's key insight is that all people have talents and important, purposeful work to do that transcends political ideology.[12] That represents a way of achieving the civil society that Rifkin sees, correctly I think, as the source of much of the work that will occur in the future.

This work will not necessarily involve public or private sector work, but "third sector" work, as Rifkin observes. Such work may not start out as a job—it may, for example, start as a volunteer or entrepreneurial effort—but it will often end up as a self-created job, done, as Morris said, for the "pleasure of the work itself." And circumstances have led many people to pursue this direction. In a recent report, the Kaufman Foundation, which publishes an annual survey of new business creation in the United States, has seen entrepreneurship rise to its highest rate in fourteen years. And most of these new start-up businesses, according to the survey, have occurred as "lifestyle businesses" more focused on what people care about and want to do with their lives than with making a lot of money.[13] Such surveys show how we have entered an era in which people have begun to redesign work in ways that makes it more meaningful and satisfying, and at the same time, more resistant to the outside forces that have made the disappearance of well-paying jobs a reality for people around the world. That trend does not just confirm Morris's insights in *News from Nowhere*. It indicates the capability of people to take the future into their own hands, to create a better world for themselves and others, and to align the work that they need to do with the work that needs doing in the world. They are in the process of creating a more resilient economy, one more resistant to catastrophic collapse and able to withstand the shock when it does occur.

13

Fracture-Critical Politics

As the nature of work changes, so too will our politics change, in part because our political system has followed a fracture-critical pattern similar to that of our economy. The effects may manifest themselves differently, but the same exponential curve that we have seen in other fracture-critical systems exists in the U.S. political arena as well. Consider the graph that political scientists Nolan McCarty, Keith T. Poole, and Howard Rosenthal have assembled that overlays the dramatic increase in political polarization in the United States with the equally dramatic rise in income inequality, measured using the Gini index. The two lines track each other almost exactly, with a rapid rise in both beginning around 1980, with the election of Ronald Reagan as U.S. president. And that may be just what some intended.[1]

This gets back to the question of our designing our way into the disasters we now face. Some might not call the steeply increasing political polarization and income inequality a disaster at all. If you don't want government as an active agent, what better way to accomplish that than by creating gridlock through polarized political positions, as we have seen in several states as well as the U.S. government? And if you see income differences as the natural result of the free market at work, then what better indication exists of success than growing inequality? Of course, for the four-fifths of the U.S. population whose incomes have remained almost unchanged, after adjustment for inflation, since the 1970s, that political gridlock and

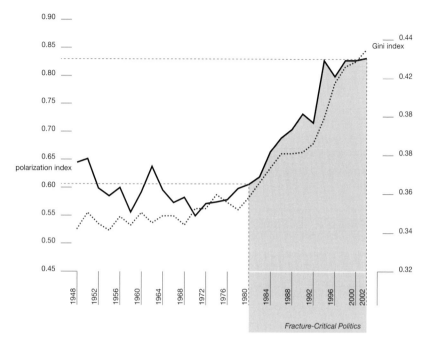

Figure 13.1 The U.S. political system has followed a fracture-critical pattern similar to that of the economy, with exponential increases in political polarization and income inequality making the system vulnerable to failure. Taking political advantage of envy, anger, and greed may work in the short term, but it is disastrous over the long term.

income inequality, which has mainly benefited the top 1 percent of U.S. citizens, certainly feels like a catastrophe.[2] In some ways, this situation mirrors the global political situation, in which the majority of the human population remains mired in poverty and unable to change their conditions appreciably because of a lack of global political will, even as those at the top have had unprecedented prosperity. Success for a few has brought disaster for most.

Such a situation remains highly unstable politically. As we have seen in other fracture-critical systems like this, such exponential stress on a highly interconnected and informationally efficient political system threatens to bring the whole thing down. And people seem aware of this, as we see in public opinion polls that show how U.S. citizens have become increasingly gloomy about their future. As a Pew Research Center/Smithsonian poll reveals, while a majority of Americans remain basically optimistic, people's pessimism about life for themselves and their families doubled between 1999 and 2010, while pessimism about the future of the United States increased by a third. Polls showing declining trust of politicians generally reinforce the sense of frustration and pessimism among a historically optimistic population.[3] The real issue lies in how the current political situation will change: suddenly and without much warning, as often happens when we ignore the signs of impending collapse, or slowly and relatively less painfully, when we acknowledge those signs and begin to change.

Those at the top of such exponential curves will often think themselves immune from such threats, but as we saw when the I-35W Bridge went down, rich and poor went down with it. And as we have seen with Ponzi schemes such as Madoff's, the well-to-do suffer disproportionately during such falls, depending upon how much they have invested in the system as it stands. Here, the old adage that the higher they are, the harder they fall does seem to apply in cases like this. Certainly the stress on the system has been building for a long time.

In 1958, economist John Kenneth Galbraith noted in his book *The Affluent Society* that ours had become a nation after World War II that accepted "private affluence" and "public squalor" as the norm.[4] In such a cultural milieu, investment in public infrastructure could not keep up with the rapid growth in private wealth in this country. That, in turn, put governments under increasing pressure to do as much as they could as efficiently as possible, given the relative lack of money available for all that we wanted done. The paradox here is that, at the very moment America could have afforded the very best infrastructure in the world, we decided, instead, to direct far more wealth into private hands and to begin to squeeze the public realm of funds. The elimination of redundancy and the dramatic increase in the interconnectedness and efficiency of our infrastructure became one of the ways in which we managed this paradox, as we tried to get as much capacity for as little public investment as possible.

A broader shift in American culture probably had some effect as well. As many commentators and critics have observed, the United States emerged from World War II not only as the leading economic and military power in the world, but also as a nation with a great deal of hubris, the excessive pride and arrogance that, as ancient Greek dramatists knew, can lead to the downfall of those who have the most to gain as well as the most to lose.[5] We now know, of course, that our enemies as well as our allies in World War II have proven to be very good competitors and that we can no longer take our dominant position since 1945 for granted. But in the decades immediately following the war, the elimination of redundancy and our pursuit of efficiency in our infrastructure expressed an over-confidence in our technological prowess that the winning of World War II seemed to instill.

All of this indicates the shaky structure upon which those at the top of the income curve have built their power. As economist Clyde Prestowitz puts it, "for some time now our 'best and brightest' have been invoking false doctrines that are systematically undermining American prosperity. Leading among these is the economic ortho-doxy of market fundamentalism, simplistic pure free trade, and hands-off government that . . . has paralyzed common sense in dealing with competitive realities."[6] Now widely recognized, that hollowing out of the American economy suggests that we have not only taken all of the redundancy out of the public infrastructure, but also taken all of the apparent private wealth in our midst for granted, as if it were real. It's as if we have purposefully under-designed the bridge we are on, but painted it to look stronger and more stable than it really is, even as we over-burden it and under-estimate its vulnerability. And when we look at the plot of the Gini index, which measures inequality and on which the United States ranks as the most unequal highly developed country in the world, we see the same exponential curve we have seen in other fracture-critical systems, in this case because relatively few people control most of the wealth and most people control relatively little.[7]

Amidst all of this, it seems as if we continue to fight twentieth-century political battles while facing twenty-first century challenges. We obviously cannot continue to starve the public sector or over-inflate the private sector without it catching up with us—rich and poor alike. Meanwhile, this century has a different character, one in which an interconnected web, rather than a set of polarized silos, has become a metaphor for reality. What we now need is not political stagnation and growing income inequality, but a much more fluid, adaptable, web-like system that can respond to diverse needs differently, sometimes with private-sector solutions and sometimes

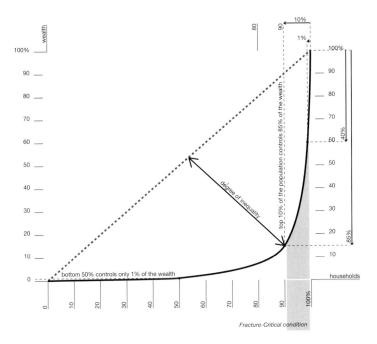

Figure 13.2 Increasing Gini coefficient due to increasing inequality. With rising inequality around the world and with the United States, the richest country in the world, having become the most unequal among its economic peers, we face a future of great instability, as we have seen with the overthrow of some Arab governments that have ignored inequality for too long.

with hybrid solutions involving public, private, and non-profit sectors. In that context, the rigid ideologies that have led to political polarization and the false affluence that has led to the global debt crisis seem simply stupid and self-defeating.

We need, instead, a much smarter way forward, one that recognizes the self-interest and self-delusion that has underpinned the intransigence and inequality of the past. This may not happen through regular channels, so clotted and confused have they become. Instead, it will most likely happen from unexpected quarters, from the youth who have inherited the mess that the twentieth-century generations have handed them, via information networks and social media that even those in power remain powerless to stop. Let us hope that the public's willingness to go along with the twentieth-century charade in U.S. politics collapses long before we witness the collapse of the system itself.

14

Reimagining Government

What would a flexible, web-like way of governing involve, one more resilient to the external shocks and unexpected disasters that have come and will continue to come with ever-greater frequency? Again, thinking about a political unit—a neighborhood, a city, a region—as a set of ecological patches might help us get past the silo-like way in which we often now organize government, like many large organizations, public and private. The typical organizational chart of such organizations has a hierarchical pyramid with the leader at the top and a cascading number of units and people below, often divided according to the specialized activities they perform.

In the web-like way in which we need to operate in the future, such hierarchies and specialized silos make little sense. First, the leaders belong at the bottom, not the top, as governance in the twenty-first century will need to have a more Tao-like character.[1] Leaders need not be at the top or in the front, commanding others to follow them into the fray; even the military rarely works that way anymore. Instead, leaders need to be among their colleagues, out ahead sometimes, following the lead of others at other times, and always seeking ways of facilitating the effort of people, while removing the unnecessary obstacles from their path so that they can do the best work possible. And leaders themselves need to model the behavior they want to see in others, doing rank-and-file work as well as visionary work, excelling in some aspect of what the organization does as well as constantly touting the excellent work of others.

That non-hierarchical form of leadership does not mean that leaders do not take responsibility for the whole. They must. But rather than see themselves at the top of a hierarchical pyramid, twenty-first century leaders need to re-imagine themselves as nodes in a web, critical to the healthy operation of the whole and essential to its response to an outside threat or opportunity, but otherwise remaining one among many. Healthy ecosystems operate in this way. Every species in it contributes to the whole and no one species dominates the others; indeed, when that domination occurs and one part of the system commands and controls all the others, the ecosystem becomes not only unhealthy, but lacking in resilience and likely to fail.[2]

Sustainable organizations, like sustainable ecosystems, require leaders who build strong networks both within and without the entity they are a part of and strive to make everyone a node in the web, with as many links to other nodes as possible. Like the brain, whose resiliency lies in the redundancy of its neural connections, the smart organization understands why nature has organized itself in this way, to ensure that that every part remains linked, able to contribute, and empowered to adapt to changes in creative and responsive ways. As in an ecosystem or in the human imagination, the best ideas for how to move in a new direction rarely come from one place in the system. Instead, they often come from many and unexpected places, and good governance recognizes and rewards that.

The web-like structure inside an organization also applies at larger scales. Just as a governing entity needs to see its own internal structure as an ecological web, so too does it need to see the community it governs in that way. This seems easier to do, since many healthy communities already have multiple networks of committees, individuals, and groups who volunteer, participate, and even self-organize in order to accomplish something that at least some in the community think important. Good governance has long involved the encouragement of such community webs, the recognition of the value they create, and an appropriate responsiveness to their recommendations.

Such webs, however, can also help get us past the gridlock and inequality that has stymied efforts to move communities forward. For instance, taxing and spending has become one of the great stumbling blocks around which so much political polarization has occurred. The old twentieth-century debate has conservatives against more taxation and government spending, and liberals for it. In the U.S. Congress, those positions have become so hardened that conservative members will not vote for a tax increase no matter what, perhaps out of fear of being ousted from or opposed in the next election by their own political party.[3] Such a hard-and-fast division does not exist in nature or in webs of any sort, and it shows how out of sync U.S. politics has become with the twenty-first century.

Instead of a "survival of the fittest" perception of nature, we now recognize the cooperative and interdependent aspects of species in ecosystems, even among predators and prey.[4] From that perspective, the winner-take-all, take-no-prisoners approach of so much modern politics reflects the larger fracture-critical nature of the culture and communities we have created. When one species, one political party, one interest group dominates, the system fails. Instead, we need to design strategies that promote win–win, non-polarizing practices able to move communities forward in environmentally sustainable, socially viable, and economically affordable ways.

French sociologist Pierre Bourdieu usefully identified three forms of wealth: economic capital, comprising financial resources like cash and assets; cultural capital, encompassing knowledge and skills; and social capital, involving the relationships and networks among people in families and communities.[5] Much of the political argument revolves around financial capital issues—taxing and spending—although cultural issues—gay marriage, abortion, and racial prejudice—often prompt the most emotional debate. Among so many of these issues, hard lines get drawn and the win–lose, for-or-against game gets played endlessly to an ever-repeating draw. But instead of trying to out-position supposed opponents, we should see the diversity of perspectives and the multiple forms of wealth in communities as our greatest strength, not a weakness. We impoverish ourselves whenever we create a monoculture of people or opinion.

Healthy communities, enriched ones, recognize the great array of wealth they have in their midst and find ways to leverage that to its fullest. For local governments with too little financial resources to meet the needs of their citizens—an all-too common scenario—tapping the cultural and social capital of their communities becomes essential, and it also offers a way of getting past the polarized views around taxing and spending. Many communities have volunteers who help make things happen, but most places also still have a twentieth-century notion that professional public servants need to do the work that the citizens pay taxes to have done. A more resilient model would have a more fluid notion of taxation, in which people in the community willing to give their time and labor or expertise would pay lower taxes, and those not willing or able to do so would pay higher ones.

This approach becomes particularly relevant in communities facing extinction. As Judith Schalansky writes in the *Atlas of Remote Islands* about the Pacific atoll Takuu in Papua New Guinea, "Takuu will sink—next month, next year" because "the sea level is rising." The people of Takuu, she writes, "do not believe the island is sinking. They refuse to leave it. They build dykes instead, packing rocks and brushwood into wide-meshed nets and tossing them onto the shores that have been diminished."[6] While islands like Takuu may be among first casualties of climate change, they won't by any means be the last. The way in which the people of Takuu have joined together to address the possible submersion of their community can serve as a model—and even an inspiration—for the rest of us who may have more time to prepare for what climate change sends our way.

This will demand that everyone in a community engages in public service of some sort, through their contribution of social capital (labor), cultural capital (expertise), or financial capital (taxes), which would vary according to the capabilities and capacities of each person. At the same time, professional public servants would become more facilitators of and advisors to the contributions of others rather than the individuals expected to do more and more work on a stagnant or declining tax base. Social critic Ivan Illich addressed this when he wrote that, "professional groups . . . have come to exert a 'radical monopoly' on such basic human activities as health, agriculture, home-building, and learning . . . The result of much economic development is very often not human flourishing but 'modernized poverty,' dependency, and an out-of-control system in which the humans become worn-down mechanical parts."[7]

Resilience comes through the ability of every member of a community to contribute in various ways. In the case of an emergency or in the case of dramatic changes in the economic conditions of a place, everyone plays a part in finding a solution or in contributing to the whole, each in their own way. No more carping from the sidelines or begrudging every penny paid for services people nevertheless expected to be there. The redesign of government comes with the admission or, in the case of some, the revelation that we are the government and the government is us. And being a part of a community comes with the demand that we participate in and contribute our time and energy to it, or else that we pay dearly for not doing so. This, in turn, alters the debate about taxes in a way that cuts across the typical party lines. Every citizen would have a choice as to what mix of capital—social, cultural, or financial—they want to contribute, but all have to contribute to the same degree, with everyone's time and ideas as valued as their money. In resilient communities, their members do what needs to get done, and the sooner we put in place public policies that put that into practice, the sooner we will have a government that works for everyone.

Fracture-Critical Higher Education

15

You have only to read a few issues of *The Chronicle of Higher Education*, one of the highest quality and least known newspapers in the United States, to understand the seemingly fragile state many colleges and universities find themselves in.[1] Governments have been cutting back their financial support of higher education, which has affected the base budgets of public institutions and the research budgets of both public and private universities. At the same time, for-profit operations have begun to grow rapidly, offering degrees for much less money and with more online convenience than traditional non-profit institutions can. This has led to the perfect financial storm of cuts causing tuition to rise and competition creating downward pressure on tuition at the same time.

Coincident with this, or perhaps in part because of it, we have seen a growing skepticism about academic expertise and academic life among growing numbers of politicians and the public at large. That anti-intellectualism, as the historian Richard Hofstadter documented, has long existed, at least in the United States, and it appears to have reared its ugly head again in recent years with the rise of populist and "know-nothing" political and social movements.[2] The sad irony of this is that at the very moment when higher education has become even more important in order for individuals and nations to compete in the global economy, some sizable sectors of the U.S. population have entered a period of dismissing academics.

We see politicians who think they know more than climatologists about climate change and pundits who think they know more than economists about debt ceilings.[3] And while we have always had uninformed people, their ability to command so much attention and to confuse so much of the public with their blather has never been greater—not a winning competitive strategy, needless to say.

Nor have the anti-intellectuals stopped with colleges and universities. One of the most pathetic features of the current political culture, again mainly in the United States, involves the spite leveled at primary and secondary school teachers by conservative politicians. Here we have a population that depends upon these same teachers to educate our children to reach their fullest potential, something that every parent wants even if they don't always have access to the quality education their children deserve, while we begrudge the meager pay teachers receive. For a state like Wisconsin, once known for valuing education, to strip its teachers of their collective bargaining rights only drives away all of the talented teachers from the state and discourages the best and the brightest students from wanting to become teachers themselves.[4] Again, this is not a formula for success.

This hostility reflects not only anti-intellectualism, but also a misguided notion of efficiency, inappropriately applied to education. We all know—as current or former students—that enlightenment does not happen on cue and that insight does not follow the clock. We all learn at our own pace and in our own way, and demanding that that occur with the same efficiency as an assembly line or routine office work seems both impractical and unachievable. The irony here is that education has long served as a counterweight to efficiency of the market, even as we teach students skills that will equip them to succeed in the market.

That counterweighting role goes back to the very beginning of higher education in the West. Socrates, whose questioning in the marketplace of Athens made people uncomfortable and eventually led to his being put to death, had an enormous influence on Plato's establishment of the first academy in order to create a "safe place for philosophy," a place beyond the reach of either the government or the marketplace.[5] That separateness became even more visible in the medieval university. As the sociologist Elliott Krause has observed, the medieval guilds—including the "guild" of academics—served as important organizations at a time when both the state and the marketplace remained relatively disorganized and certainly much weaker than they are today.[6] Aspects of modern universities, such as tenure and accreditation, reflect those roots in the middle ages and such academic policies reveal the extent to which the guilds not only organized the work of their members, but also controlled the quality of work and longevity of workers.

That situation has largely reversed itself in today's world. Another remnant of the medieval guilds—today's unions—have become much weakened, at least in the United States, as both government and businesses have become so dominant in our lives. At first, the rise of the state and of capitalistic activity benefited universities, which have become training grounds for both public and private leaders as well as centers for research on matters of public or private interest. But in recent decades, as the political parties that favor either big government or big businesses have brought aspects of state and federal governance almost to a halt, the value of private-sector efficiency has become a primary measure of effectiveness. This has led to the almost constant drumbeat from the party of big business to reduce the size and expense of big government, pointing to the latter's supposed inefficiency when compared to the market-place. That democratic institutions are *supposed* to be inefficient, in a business sense, tends to get lost in the political debates; if people want efficient government, they should go live in a dictatorship.

Similar misguided measures have also had a negative effect on educational institutions. A complaint heard by some critics revolves around the question of tenure: if the marketplace doesn't need tenure, why should education? The answer takes us back to the very first academy, which Plato started in order to protect people asking good questions that made the powerful uncomfortable. Without such protections, the free and open marketplace of ideas—so essential to human progress and improvements to our quality of life—would quickly become the marketplace of whatever those in power deemed acceptable or advantageous. Again, we have only to look at closed societies, in which dictators rule, to see what the prohibition of "dangerous" ideas does to the standard of living and quality of life of ordinary people.

The fracture-critical nature of modern education lies not in the structure and organization of schools, colleges, and universities. The latter, in particular, have proven to be among the most durable and resilient institutions of Western culture, with several universities in Europe, along with entities like the Catholic Church, among the only medieval institutions that continue to thrive to this day. The danger of catastrophic collapse comes, instead, from the undermining of education from outside, by those who have an almost evangelical belief that everything should work like the marketplace and who misapply metrics from that realm to judge negatively every other realm that doesn't fit that mold.

The sad irony of this is that these evangelical capitalists do not see that the business world has thrived precisely because our government and our educational institutions have not mimicked the marketplace. Good government—healthy democratic government— has ensured the level playing fields, the protections for consumers, and the prosecution of cheaters that allow honest competition in the marketplace to occur. And the same has happened in education. Tenure policies and accreditation standards have ensured that we ask the difficult questions that help us discover new knowledge and develop new strategies and technology in a context that guarantees the quality of the people, processes, and procedures necessary to do this work as well as possible. Without such protections and assurances—without independent government watchdogs and independent researchers and scholars in the academy—not only would the political and educational systems that have been so crucial to our quality of life collapse, but capital markets would collapse with them. No one wants that.

16

Redesigning the University

That said, there is always room for improvement, and so how might higher education, in particular, change with the times to ensure its continued relevance in a world that is itself changing in dramatic ways? Some of the most promising transformations that might occur echo forms of education that used to exist and that we would do well to revisit and possibly repurpose in new ways. Here, as in so many other aspects of building a more resilient future for ourselves, the solutions, while different from what we have done in the immediate past, often arise from older forms of human activity, making the resiliency movement at once progressive and conservative, forward thinking and backward looking at the same time. What's past, as Shakespeare said, is prologue.

Many possible scenarios exist for the future form of the university, but four seem particularly promising and have already begun to happen. The first scenario involves a conversation-based university, echoing that of the Greco-Roman part of our past. In the information age, where students have ample and immediate access to large amounts of data, education has become much less about lecturing and the one-way delivery of knowledge and much more about helping students critically assess information and engaging them in a discussion about its meaning. As in the Socratic tradition of learning, the future university may be much more conversational, and simultaneously wireless and mobile.

The design studio provides one model of this "conversation theory," as Gordon Pask famously described it.[1] There, faculty guide and challenge individual students in an iterative and intense way, based on the information and insights that students bring to their work. The physical form of the studio also suggests a new kind of space for conversation-based learning, one in which there would be less specialized, structured space and a much greater diversity of informal work environments supported by digital technology. This might serve as a model for higher education in an age of information overload, where learning involves finding the meaning of all that data and trying to make a meaningful difference in the world.

A second way in which universities have begun to change has come with the rise of distance education. This echoes the medieval condition in which education occurred in a much more fluid and decentralized way. While organizations like the University of Phoenix represent one example of what distance learning might be, there exist many more online, part-time, and just-in-time ways of delivering knowledge to people where they are and when they need it, all of which transcend the physical constraints of the university campus.

While it will likely never replace in-person education, distance learning will become increasingly important as we face the need to educate large percentages of the global population in ways that are affordable and accessible, as well as the need to drive new types of revenue into colleges and universities.[2] This placeless form of education still has a form and understanding the environments best suited to the different forms of knowledge delivery remains an important task before us. The observation of Umberto Eco, novelist and linguist, that late modernism has a "neo-medieval" quality may help us as we find ourselves re-imagining the university along medieval lines, bringing education to people rather than demanding that people come to us.[3]

A third direction in which universities have begun to move involves the rise of individualized learning.[4] In contrast to the disciplinary knowledge that emerged in the early modern era, students increasingly want choice and the ability to customize their education, which challenges the assumption that we learn best in silo-like curriculums in discrete departments. It suggests, instead, a web-like, interconnected form of education in which students put together parts of several fields in response to the new opportunities and demands that they see in the world. The individualized learning programs that already exist in many institutions as an option for a relatively few students may, someday, become the norm.

The project-based learning that occurs in design studio also lends itself to this hybridized form of education. As in a design project, when students develop solutions to particular problems and respond to specific needs, individualized ways of learning may demand the use of interdisciplinary projects as a way of giving a diversity of disciplinary interests some coherence. Design, in this context, offers a way of navigating, ordering, and seeing patterns across a landscape of learning, imagined more like an ecology of knowledge rather than as a series of separate categories.

A fourth scenario that some higher education institutions have begun to embrace involves the notion of the challenge-based university, harkening back to the experiential learning that the philosopher John Dewey advocated.[5] As communities and governments face ever-more complex problems, some schools have begun to explore the idea of organizing themselves around the most pressing challenges of the day, akin to the way in which nineteenth-century research universities reorganized themselves around scientific and social problems. Students would still study a discipline, but would, at the same time, work with students and faculty from a range of fields on a particular societal challenge over the course of many years. This not only helps students ground their learning in real-world applications of it, but also helps universities respond more effectively to the interdisciplinary problems of our time, bringing together the fields necessary to address an issue in the most integrated and holistic way possible.

This, in turn, suggests new ways of thinking about the geography of knowledge at a university. There may be much less discipline-based turf in the future and much more flexible, team-based space, in which various disciplines can work together in close proximity on a common problem and then disband when they have completed a project. The campus of a challenge-based university might start to look like a project-based design firm, with workspace for the multiple disciplines on a project that come together for short periods of time and then disperse.

In all four of these scenarios, creative thinking will play an increasingly important role. Colleges and universities have reached a point where tweaking the old system no longer works, evident in the unsustainable rise in student tuition and the ongoing decline in public support. As with so many of the fracture-critical threats we now face, higher education needs several paradigm shifts in how it operates, educates, and organizes itself, making universities one of the major design problems of our time. This is important not only to re-invigorate these resilient institutions so that they can do a better job of educating a much more diverse range of students, but also to engage the best minds we have in the tremendous problems we face as a species living on this planet.

Roger Martin, dean at the University of Toronto's Rotman School of Business, argues that design thinkers need to be at the corporate boardroom table, helping companies think creatively and strategically.[6] The same thing needs to happen at colleges and universities. Design thinkers, creative and practical problem solvers, need to be at the table not just to help plan new buildings or to landscape the campus, but also to apply the future-oriented, conceptually based scenario-building that remains the most valuable aspect of design. Such thinking has helped universities redesign themselves in the past, as the demands on them and the contexts around them changed, and the time has come to do so again.

17

Fracture-Critical Infrastructure

Fracture-critical infrastructures, like the I-35W Bridge, remain highly visible when they collapse. Most of the infrastructure we depend on in our daily lives, however, exists out of sight, below ground or in such a distributed pattern that we often don't think about it. We assume that when we switch on the lights or put a plug into a socket, electricity stands at the ready to power what we want to happen, or that when we turn a faucet or start a shower, clean water will come. Likewise, when we operate a lawnmower or automobile, that we will have access to oil or gas when we need it to replenish what we use. Such activities have become such an expected part of modern life, the result of infrastructure that we have much to be proud of given the complexity of delivering so much to so many people across such a great distance, that we can easily overlook its lack of redundancy and its vulnerability to massive failure as a result.

New Orleans's levee system serves as an easily understood example of what fracture-critical infrastructure looks like. While Hurricane Katrina certainly stressed that system with high winds and waves, the flooding of the city came after the hurricane had begun to subside. The levees, weakened by the storm, gave way in a few places, but rather than flood a relatively small area near the breaks in the wall, polluted water inundated most of the city, turning an initially minor failure into a catastrophe.[1] This was no "natural" disaster. It resulted from the same error in thinking that led to the I-35W Bridge collapse and that has led to the series of failures we have had to deal with in recent years. While no one intentionally designed the New Orleans levee system to cause such catastrophic damage, we did not design it to ensure that it would not happen either.

We cannot, of course, guarantee that nothing will ever go wrong or foresee every possible event in what we design; everything in life always has an element of risk. But we have, over the last century, designed systems as if nothing would go wrong or as if everything would be done to maintain them so that they would not fail. Our justifiable pride in and optimism about technology—about our ability to find a means or mechanism to solve almost every problem we face—has perhaps prevented us from making a realistic assessment of our financial capacity and political will to keep up infrastructure and to maintain it in perfect working order. In theory, the New Orleans levee system should not have failed, but in fact, years of deferred maintenance, temporary fixes, and antiquated equipment made its failure almost inevitable.

Had we envisioned that critical piece of New Orleans infrastructure with the reality of cutbacks, shortfalls, and deferrals in mind, we might have created a less fracture-critical system. We would not have had only one line of defense between the water and the entire city, with no redundant layer of levee walls and no alternative route for the water to follow until the break could be repaired. The city depended entirely on the efficient and highly interconnected levees continuing to stand, with pumps as the main backup should water overtop the walls—a backup system clearly incapable of handling the floodwaters once the levees failed. At the same time, the connectedness of all parts of the city created a condition in which a levee break at any point led to the inundation of neighborhoods far from the breach. The difference between a flawed design and a fracture-critical one rests there: not only in its vulnerability to failure, but also in the catastrophic consequences once that happens, affecting a much wider area or much larger number at a much greater cost than anyone anticipated.

The nation's electrical grid offers another example of fracture-critical infrastructure, whose failure would affect a far greater number of people than in post-Katrina New Orleans. On August 15, 2003, a local power failure near Cleveland cascaded into the largest power failure in North American history, leaving fifty million people in large portions of the United States and Canada without power for days and causing an estimated $10 billion in damages.[2] Five years after the blackout, industry experts worry that the situation has gotten worse rather than better, with excess capacity in the electrical power grid declining and demand for electricity by 2030 expected to increase 29 percent on 2006 levels.[3]

This exemplifies the kind of fracture-critical system we need to attend to immediately. One failure can bring large sections of the system down, affecting a huge number of people and causing damage that costs far more than the expense of adding capacity and of building in redundancy and firewalls to contain a failure to a local area. In an era of terrorism, in which a few people look for opportunities to create the most chaos and alarm as easily as possible, our fracture-critical electrical grid also lends itself to sabotage, making the added cost of a more resilient system an even better investment.

The irony here lies in the contrast between the electrical grid, vulnerable to cascading, catastrophic failure, and the electronic web of technology that depends on this grid for its power. The Internet has a highly resilient form, with an extraordinary amount of redundancy because of the myriad servers and devices that link to it and convey information along the system. At a meta-level, though, it has the same vulnerability as the power grid upon which it depends: without electricity, the web doesn't work. Resilient systems, in other words, cannot exist in a vacuum. Unless redundancy and resistance to sudden failure occur at multiple scales, the system remains as vulnerable as its weakest link. The lack of resilience at one scale can cancel out an abundance of it at another, particularly if the fracture-critical system exists at a larger scale or in support of the more resilient one.

This reveals the self-defeating quality of "the tragedy of the commons" as ecologist Garrett Hardin first described it.[4] The tragedy

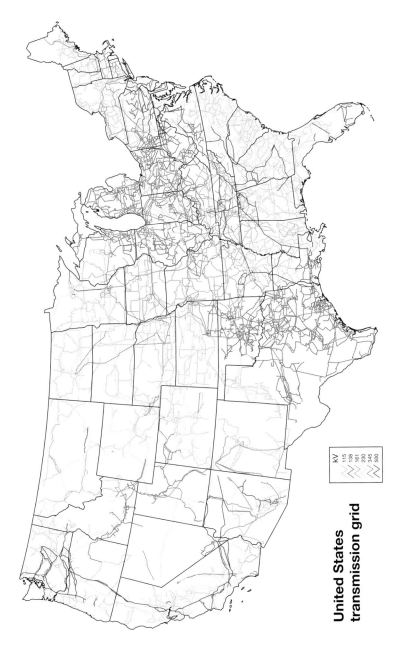

United States transmission grid

KV
115
138
161
230
345
500

Figure 17.1 The U.S. electrical power grid epitomizes the country's fracture-critical infrastructure, in which a few transmission stations affect the performance of the whole and in which failure along many parts of the system can bring down large segments of it.

occurs when people or organizations try to maximize personal benefits by exploiting shared resources like unpolluted air, clean water, and healthy ecosystems, while shifting the cost of the damage as much as possible to others, be they fellow taxpayers, future generations, distant populations, or other species. What makes this tragic is the shortsightedness of those who attempt this exploitation. While it seems wise to maximize gain and minimize costs, with enough people doing the same, the commons becomes so degraded that no one can exploit it any further without completely destroying it and threatening all who depend on it, including those who exploited it in the first place. Add to that the tipping-point quality of most systems, in which a slight increase in stress on an already overstressed entity can lead to sudden and surprising shifts, and we begin to see how the tragedy of the commons becomes a form of collective Russian roulette, with the loaded gun aimed at us all.

We can get past this tragedy not by privatizing the commons as conservatives have argued or highly regulating it as liberals might like, but instead by recognizing that we all exist, like the rest of nature, in an inseparable relationship with everyone and everything else. Once we see that we can never shift costs onto others without those costs—and the consequences of our exploits—shifting right back onto us, then the debate about privatization or public control becomes rather irrelevant. We all exist and depend on one planet and so everything we do to it and to each other invariably affects each one of us and all of us at the same time. Timing is the issue here. While most of us know that we all breathe the same air, for example, those who would exploit that air by polluting often think that they can get away with it over a long enough timeframe that they will not have to pay the true cost of their actions.

But on a planet where the atmosphere is about as thick as a coat of shellac, were the earth the size of a basketball, there is no time lag to pollution.[5] We breathe in what we spew out almost immediately, and so the tragedy of the commons is really the tragedy of human ignorance and self-defeating behavior. Unless we account for the sustainability and resiliency of things at every scale—the parts that comprise our whole and the larger whole of which ours remains a part—we will remain vulnerable to catastrophic failures. No amount of new technology or better engineering will make us less susceptible to disaster unless we also start to think differently about our relationship to the world around us. The earth will do just fine without us. It is we who cannot live without the earth, and so rethinking this relationship isn't about altruism. It's about survival.

18

Going Dutch

The slang term "going Dutch" refers to the etiquette of sharing equally in paying for something on a date with another person or when out socializing with a group of people. We have probably all "gone Dutch" sometime in our lives, and yet rarely do we apply that principle to life itself: taking care of things ourselves rather than depending upon others to pay for us, living within our means rather than way beyond them. As the philosopher René Descartes wrote, while living in Holland, "[I] try always to conquer myself rather than fortune, and to alter my desires rather than change the order of the world"—a maxim that underlies the social courtesy of "going Dutch" as we alter our own desires to fit what we have the ability to pay for ourselves.[1] But in the designed world upon which we depend, we have continually tried to change the order of the world rather than our own desires, leading the most affluent portion of humanity to live way beyond what we can afford.

Look at how the Dutch have dealt with some of the same systems that have become so vulnerable to failure in the United States. Like New Orleans, a sizable portion of Holland lies below sea level, and it, too, struggles to ensure the stability of its system of dikes. But unlike the levees around New Orleans, in which one break led to the flooding of large parts of the city, the Dutch have divided their land into smaller "polders"—some 3,000 in all—so that if a dike fails, the flood damage remains minimal, avoiding the catastrophic failure of a fracture-critical system, as happened in New Orleans.[2]

The Dutch also use local materials in the construction of many of their dikes, allowing for continual repair if signs of weakening occur and minimizing the cost of such repair when needed. That resiliency also contrasts with the large-scale and high-cost repair and maintenance requirements of the New Orleans system, whose very expense led to the deferred maintenance that ultimately contributed to the levees' failure. The irony of fracture-critical systems, often justified because of their efficient use of materials and lower first cost, lies in their demand for far more money over time in repair and maintenance, and in the extreme costliness of repairing the damage and replacing the system if—and when—it fails.

The Dutch levee system suggests some principles that we would do well to learn as we face the task of designing a more resilient infrastructure for ourselves. We need to reduce the scale and increase the diversity of the systems on which we depend. This runs counter to the idea that has driven our infrastructure for the last century, which has focused on centrally controlled, national-scale systems such as the levees along our rivers put in place by the Army Corps of Engineers. We have tended to see strength in uniformity and large scale, when in fact such systems—unless they have incredible redundancy—end up also causing uniformly large-scale damage when they fail. The smaller the scale and more diverse the system, the less likely any one failure will endanger more than a few or prove too costly to repair, as the Dutch have learned.

We also need to base our systems on local materials and capabilities. This follows from the previous point, since a more locally based infrastructure will, as a matter of course, have more diverse and smaller-scale units. This, too, comes up against the dominant idea of the recent past of using the newest materials and the biggest technology, when in fact the resiliency of a system increases when a community can construct, maintain, and even repair its own infrastructure without having to wait for the newest and biggest to arrive from some far-off, central location.

Nor can we see our infrastructure apart from the larger community of which it remains a part. Our resiliency depends not just on the design of the physical systems we depend on, but also on the development of social systems that ensure the long-term maintenance of critical infrastructure. The Dutch teach their children about their polders and how to maintain and repair them, distributing responsibility for the system across the entire population rather than in a single, governmental agency. The Dutch have also aligned their land policies and development strategies with the polder system, so that property boundaries as well as the location of buildings and roads coincide with the dike locations, so that the whole works in concert with the parts and vice versa.

As we have begun to rebuild New Orleans, such thinking remains hardly in evidence. Homeowners in that city have begun to return to their properties and rebuild their houses, as the Army Corps of Engineers has reinforced the levees and begun to make up for the years of deferred maintenance on the system. But the design flaw that led to the catastrophe after Hurricane Katrina remains in place, waiting for the disaster to happen again.[3] A more resilient rebuilding of the city would have a much more redundant levee system, with multiple layers and discrete sections so that a future break in a wall would inundate only a relatively small part of the whole. Likewise, private structures and public infrastructure would expect possible flooding, with occupied space and essential services elevated above the high-water mark and accessible even after a flood has occurred, possibly from elevated roads like those that exist throughout Holland. We know how to do such things. But until we start designing our environments to handle the worst possible situation and greatest imaginable failure, we will continue to spend far more money and endanger far more lives and livelihoods than we need to, not just in rare situations like New Orleans, but in one community after another, each vulnerable in its own way to some force of nature or some unexpected failure of infrastructure.

The British Petroleum oil spill in the Gulf of Mexico shows what we risk in ignoring that design principle.[4] As the search for oil has become desperate with the demand for this resource starting to outstrip the supply, oil companies have started to drill in ever-deeper waters and to push for ever-faster results. That combination of greater difficulty combined with more speed, when graphed, gets us right back to the rapidly rising curve we have seen in fracture-critical situations before. The risk and costliness of a failure increases exponentially as we push technology past previous limits, into ever-more dangerous situations, even as we expect everything to work perfectly. Let the oil spill serve to mark the extent and depth not only of our technological prowess, but also of our unsustainable hubris.

A more humble approach to the world would also ensure a less disastrous one. Instead of drilling one deep well and depending upon one piece of equipment—a "blow-out preventer"—to prevent a $20-billion-dollar-plus disaster, we might require every oil company to drill two wells to every reserve, so that, if one "preventer" fails to avert a disaster, the back-up well would relieve the pressure enough to allow the capping of the first well. This sounds inefficient, like having a belt and suspenders when, in most cases, one or the other will do. But the cost of our supposed efficiency has become so great, and the damage our systems can cause so severe, that the most reasonable approach would have us do whatever it takes to prevent a disaster from happening in the first place.

The belt-and-suspenders approach applies to organizational resiliency as well. The Royal Dutch Shell Company, one of the world's largest oil companies, and the Dutch utility Nuon have started building wind-turbine farms off Holland's coast among sixty-five wind-farm sites identified by the Dutch government.[5] The private and public sectors, working together, reduce the risk to both and ensure a mutually reinforcing approach to system design, something hard to achieve in the United States, with its polarization of the private and the public sector. Ideology can have as much of a fracture-critical nature as any bridge or bulwark. While seemingly strong, ideologies can collapse just as suddenly in the face of a reality that doesn't fit the fictions that ideologues often promote.

The best way to handle the overwhelmed electrical grid in the United States involves creating as many different sources and as many distributed systems as possible.[6] Dismissing wind or solar technologies because they cannot generate enough power represents fracture-critical thinking at its best, or worst. Having solar and wind power contribute what they can to our electrical needs, and valuing that contribution at a time when the environmental damage of other fuels like coal or oil has come at a cost we can no longer ignore, makes the building of wind and solar-collector farms a critically important task. Likewise, removing obstacles to individuals and organizations generating and storing their own power adds to the resiliency of the whole. The infrastructure we need to create has multiple, diverse systems at a range of scales, each contributing in its own way and to the greatest extent possible to the larger whole, while containing as many diverse parts and renewable features as possible.

Our ancestors, who put the sun, wind, and water to wonderfully creative uses, understood this all too well. Once we stop believing in the myth that our generations have more intelligence than those of the past, we will begin to rediscover the remarkable insights of those who have preceded us, able to design and build whatever they needed from what they had at hand, with great subtlety and sophistication and without the brute-force—and sometimes bone-headed—approach that we have taken to do essentially the same thing. Imagine a world in which we lived within the limits of what the sun and soil, wind and water had to give us for free. That is the resilient, resourceful, and resolute environment human beings once occupied and that we can occupy again if we can learn, as Descartes did, to alter our desires rather than to keep trying to change the planet.

19

Fracture-Critical Developments

Infrastructure remains a relatively abstract idea, something that most people not only do not see, but also do not have much of an opportunity to affect in our daily lives. So let's look at another fracture-critical system literally closer to home: our housing system. In the United States, a larger percentage of the housing built after World War II occurred in the suburbs, where builders constructed homes at a mass scale, often in developments in which the houses all had generally the same price point, the same target market, and frequently the same set of roughly similar plans.[1] These large tract developments proved efficient to build, with assembly line processes like those used in the making of military equipment during World War II, where crews would do the same operation—framing, finishing, roofing—in one nearly identical house after another. The color of the exterior, the orientation of the roof, or the nature of the trim might vary from one house to the next, but the similarities among them lowered construction costs and reduced the cost of the houses to consumers.

The scale of these suburban developments, with so many comparable houses immediately adjacent, made it easy for the developers to finance, city inspectors to review, and real estate agents to sell. These architectural monocultures also ensured that homeowners would have neighbors like themselves, reducing the apparent risk of taking on a mortgage and of relying on the value of the property to appreciate. The power of those incentives, combined with the leverage of buying a house mostly on credit, deducting the mortgage interest from one's income taxes, and receiving the benefits of government-backed loans and government-led investments in infrastructure, made the move to suburbia by all who could afford it irresistible and almost inevitable.

We have since discovered, though, how much the efficiency and apparent security of these suburban developments made them fracture-critical in an unexpected way. When homeowners default on their mortgages and get foreclosed upon, banks will typically lower the price of the house in order to sell quickly to recoup some of their losses. But if enough foreclosures occur in a development in which the other houses have essentially the same design, the value of all the properties will fall, often to the point where many homeowners find themselves "underwater," paying more for their mortgages than their houses are worth. This, in turn, creates an incentive for more homeowners to walk away and more banks to foreclose, which creates a downward spiral that can lead to the economic collapse of an entire neighborhood.[2] As in the I-35W Bridge, a few cracks in the market value of the homes in a homogenous community and the average prices in the whole place come crashing down.

Many people have blamed Federal tax breaks for fueling the housing bubble and the subsequent foreclosure crisis that occurred after the bubble burst in 2007.[3] But sub-prime mortgages designed to get as many people as possible into their own houses—and designed to maximize as much as possible lenders' profits and minimize their risk—lie at the heart of the housing bubble's bursting.[4] Creating products that not only failed at such a massive scale, but that also brought down the very companies that sold them, represents the epitome of bad design. But few people have looked at how the design of the developments themselves has also contributed to the situation. Too much of the same thing, too close together, without enough diversity of all sorts—types, sizes, function—sets the stage for collapse.

The location of housing can make it as vulnerable as its mix. A growing population combined with the low-density sprawl that has

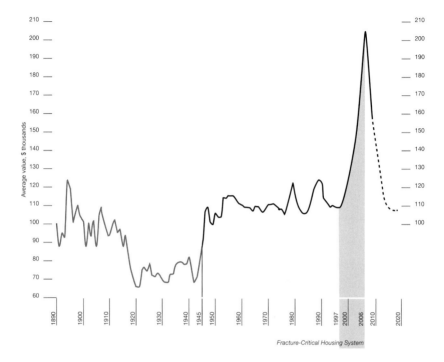

Figure 19.1 A History of U.S. home values. Many Americans moved to suburban tract developments thinking that the economic and ethnic uniformity of such places helped protect their investment. It turns out, though, that that uniformity also makes the prices of houses in such developments vulnerable to collapse when enough houses go into foreclosure.

characterized development especially since World War II had led to housing increases occurring in areas once thought foolish—or even dangerous—to live in. Consider the amount of prime farmland near population centers that has disappeared beneath the crab grass of suburban developments. Pushing our food sources further and further away seems the opposite of what every other animal on this planet would do. Or consider locations vulnerable to forest fires, where homebuilders, developers, and owners still get permission and financing for houses in or near fire-hazard areas. In Washington State, almost half of its homes border forests or have heavy vege- tation vulnerable in forest fires, with 65 percent of those houses in "severe fire zones," and in high fire-hazard states like California, information about where the risk remains the highest doesn't even exist in a single map.[5]

A hazard more common than fire is flooding, and yet here too development continues to intrude into areas prone to inundation. The number of people living on land vulnerable to floods has increased substantially globally, with an estimated one billion people currently exposed and an expected two billion to be so by 2050.[6] Add to that the likelihood of rising sea levels and more severe storms as a result of climate change, and humanity seems headed to more catastrophes as large as or larger than the one that affected New Orleans after Katrina. In low-lying countries like Bangladesh, where a less than one-foot rise in sea level would inundate the land of thirty-three million people, the scope of destruction becomes almost unimaginable.[7]

These trends may seem inevitable: more people need more land in less desirable areas. But New Orleans shows how such fatalism has little basis in fact, since a lot of this movement into vulnerable locations has to do with the assumptions we make about how people live. Geographer Richard Campanella has shown how half of New Orleans stands at or above sea level, and that at population densities that existed up to around 1960 about 300,000 people could live above sea level: 90 percent of the city's population in 1910 and more than enough to accommodate the population in 2006, with room for 80,000 more people.[8] In other words, decreasing housing densities caused the city's population, especially since World War II, to spread into the low-lying former wetlands behind the high ground that had previously housed most—and in the nineteenth century, all—of New Orleans' population. And because of that sprawl, there remain even today a large number of open parcels on high ground, land that we should infill before another building gets constructed below sea level.

The suburbanization of cities and subsidization of sprawl in the United States and increasingly around the world has created a fracture-critical condition in terms of land use and natural (and often human-created) hazards. The New Orleans situation also shows how one vulnerability often relates to another. Had that city's population continued to develop at the density of its French Quarter, it could have accommodated its population prior to Katrina entirely above sea level and maintained the wetlands that had absorbed flooding in earlier eras. In that case, the fracture-critical levee system, with its one layer of protection, would not have mattered much, since a break in that system would have mostly inundated unpopulated areas meant to flood. A resilient system at a larger scale, in other words, can often accept a less resilient system at a smaller scale. A New Orleans designed to flood, with people living on high ground and with ample low-lying open space, can accept periodic flooding more readily, just as a housing development designed for occasional downturns, with a diversity of housing types, sizes, and costs, can handle a fall in prices more easily.

Such things do not take sophisticated technology or a suppression of our freedom to achieve. We have confused liberty with the license to do whatever an individual wants and can afford to do.[9] That libertarian way of thinking, however appealing it may seem at first glance, often ignores the fact that no one lives in a vacuum, and that we all affect and are affected by others, no matter how isolated or independent we may appear to be. Let's say the people of New Orleans had zoned their city to prohibit people living below sea level. Libertarians might argue that if a person had the money to build a house below sea level even in low-lying land and would accept the risk related to it, that person should have the right to do so. That argument, though, often overlooks the fact that the rest of us end up picking up the cost of that person's "freedom" in everything from the public services and infrastructure costs to the collective sharing in the insurance and healthcare coverage to the expense of safety and evacuation services should a catastrophic flood occur.

That illusion of absolute freedom gets compounded when such thinking becomes accepted as the norm and public pressure leads to its becoming legislated upon. The forces that encouraged the people of New Orleans to sprawl into low-lying areas — policies that favored low-density living and subsidized the infrastructure to support it — came largely from state and federal laws that have proven damaging to every city in the United States, and absolutely devastating to a city like New Orleans, where traditional higher-density development made the difference between survivability and submersion. Location, in other words, matters, and so does resisting the temptation to do really stupid things, whether it involves living in a flood or fire zone or inhabiting a development designed under the pretense that home prices only go up.

20

A Better Way to Dwell

Our ancestors knew better. For most of human history, the factors that influenced the location of human settlements remained much the same: sites suitable for settlement needed to have access to water (and the plant and animal life equally attracted to water), available resources with which to build (trees for wood, clay for brick), and protection from obvious hazards (above flood levels, away from other natural or human threats). The design of human settlements, of course, also sought to compensate for what a site didn't already offer in abundance. Communities dug wells to access water not available on the surface, traded for materials they didn't have at hand, and built protective barriers against flood, fire, or human foes. Still, there existed a limit to which people would go. Archaeologists can often identify possible settlement sites with remarkable accuracy because of their understanding of where humans typically located.[1]

The avoidance of barren, hazardous, or exposed locations by people in the past arose not only out of a fear of the danger in settling there, but also because our technology did not allow us to overcome or insulate ourselves from the risks involved. That has changed, especially over the last two hundred years, because the pace of innovation has increased exponentially along with the rise of cities, the increase in wealth, and the growth of our ecological footprint on the planet. This technological revolution has enabled us to live almost anywhere we want—in arid or arctic regions, flood or fire-prone zones, skyscrapers or suburbs — far from where humans have historically settled. And yet we have paid a price in terms of the pace of change this revolution has forced upon us, at great cost.

Bio-physicist Geoffrey West, and a group of his colleagues at the Santa Fe Institute, has equated this to the pace at which the rest of the natural world operates. They distinguish between the "sublinear scaling" of nature, in which the metabolism or pace of biological activity decreases with an increase in the mass or size of an organism and ecosystem, and "superlinear scaling" of human communities, in which the metabolism or pace increases with size, as in a city.[2]

As West writes:

The bigger the organization, the faster the pace of life. In big cities, disease spreads more quickly, business is transacted more rapidly, and people walk faster — all in approximately the same systematic, predictable way . . . To sustain such growth in the light of resource limitation requires continuous cycles of paradigm-shifting innovations . . . There is, however, a serious catch: Theory dictates that the time between successive innovations must get shorter and shorter . . . Until recent times the interval between major innovations far exceeded the productive life span of a human being. But this is no longer true: The time between the most recent major shift from computers to IT was only about 20 years and is destined to get even shorter. This pace is surely not sustainable and, if nothing changes, we are heading for a major crash — a potential collapse of the entire socioeconomic fabric. Can we return to an analogue of the sublinear, "biological" phase whence we evolved and its attendant, natural, no-growth, asymptotically stable configuration? Is this even possible?[3]

In other words, can humans return to a time, before the industrial revolution, in which we lived at a pace appropriate to our species, as our pre-machine-age ancestors did? Or are we destined to have to innovate at an ever-faster rate in order to sustain economic growth at acceptable levels and accommodate a population increasing exponentially? And is there a limit to how fast we can innovate or at

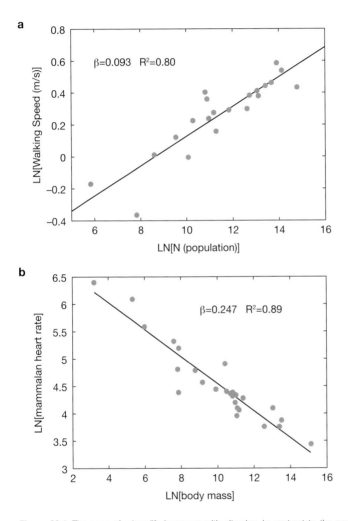

Figure 20.1 The pace of urban life increases with city size, in contrast to the pace of biological life, which decreases with organism size. The top graph shows how the speed at which people walk increases with a city's population, while the bottom graph shows how heart rate decreases with an animal's size. From the paper "Growth, innovation, scaling, and the pace of life in cities," Luis Bettencourt, José Lobo, Dirk Helbing, Christian Kühnert, and Geoffrey West, *Proceedings of the National Academy of Science*.

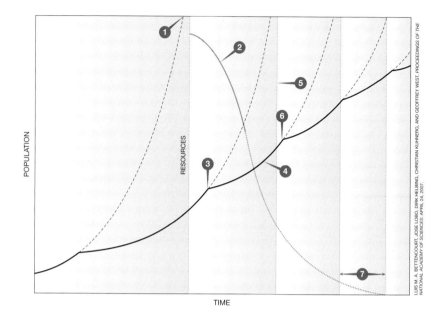

Figure 20.2 The progress of innovation (4) offers the best way of countering the exponential stress curves (1) that lead to catastrophic collapse (2). Innovations (3, 6) occur over time (5), however the pace of innovation has continually to increase (7) in order to keep up with the stresses we keep placing on our support systems, which is not sustainable. From the paper "Growth, innovation, scaling, and the pace of life in cities," Luis Bettencourt, José Lobo, Dirk Helbing, Christian Kühnert, and Geoffrey West, *Proceedings of the National Academy of Science.*

least absorb the innovations that arise? Those who claim the right and demand the freedom to do what they want typically do so with the often-unspoken assumption that we will find a technological fix for whatever obstacle or problem may occur as a result of this license to do what we have never done before. But here, too, we have to ask if limits exist to where we should settle or how we should dwell on the planet. Might the restraint of our tendency to overthrow constraints constitute one of the most important innovations we might devise?

We frequently view progress in terms of what we can now do that we couldn't before, but real progress in the future may involve, instead, the rediscovery of what humans once knew, but that we have forgotten or chosen to ignore. The great technological task we face may, in fact, constitute finding the modern "analogue of the sublinear, 'biological' phase whence we evolved," as West put it.[4] This need not involve a retreat or return to some primitive existence. Indeed, the only real guarantee of such a retreat may come from ignoring the need to do this and continuing on our current path to the "potential collapse of the entire socioeconomic fabric," as West says.[5] We need, instead, to see the challenge of relearning how to live within our biological limits as the next phase in the evolution of our species. This will take extraordinary innovation and creativity to achieve, and not just in the area of science and technology, but also in the social, intellectual, and spiritual structures we construct for ourselves.

Fortunately, history offers us all sorts of clues as to how we might accomplish this. This does not mean that anyone should have to put up with the unhealthy, noisy, and overcrowded conditions or the repressive, prejudicial, or patriarchal policies of the past; we should not forget the progress we have made in order to make a different kind of progress in the future. So what might that different kind of progress look like? It would begin with the recognition that beyond certain, very modest limits, having more doesn't get us more. Adam Smith, the father of capitalism, acknowledged that when he wrote that "the rich . . . consume little more than the poor . . . they are led by an invisible hand to make nearly the same distribution of the necessaries of life."[6] In other words, what people actually need in order to live remains roughly the same for all of us; despite variations in body size, activity, or location, people all require about the same number of calories and fluids in order to function, about the same amount of clothing in order to stay warm, and the same amount of covered space in order to keep dry. Smith saw the genius of the marketplace as lying not in making a few people rich, but in making such necessities of life available to everyone.

Not only do all human beings need approximately the same amount of food, clothing, and shelter in order to live, but also that amount, even with seven billion of us on the planet, remains within the carrying capacity of the earth. "There have been many attempts to calculate the Earth's carrying capacity for human populations," writes population expert Joel Cohen in *How Many People Can the Earth Support?* "Recent estimates range from David Pimentel's 1 to 2 billion people in relative prosperity, to the Food and Agriculture Organization's estimate of 33 billion people fed on minimum rations and using every available hectare of suitable land for high-intensity food production."[7] Such a wide range shows our confusion about what we really need. The "relative prosperity" that can accommodate only one to two billion people reflects not what a human being needs in order to thrive, but instead the trappings of modern life—the houses and cars and equipment—that we have come to equate with having a good life, even though the vast majority of our ancestors lived with much less and, from all accounts, considered themselves able to live just as happily. The expectations that we have in terms of what constitutes a good life makes all the difference, then, between our ability to sustain ourselves—or not—as a species within the carrying capacity of the planet.

If cities have always served as a source of innovation, as West observes, so too have they offered qualitative growth opportunities for individuals and communities—social and cultural activities, artistic and educational pursuits, entertainment and sporting events—that do not necessarily require more resources or more material wealth in order to enjoy. And that occurs most effectively when a great diversity of people can interact most easily. Historically, that occurred in compact settlements that had a variety of people living and working in close proximity, with most of their needs satisfied within a convenient walking distance. Such settlements will need to re-emerge, be they in large cities made up of many com- pact communities or in smaller, denser suburbs or small towns. Meanwhile their digital equivalent may also arise, in which people have access to the same opportunities while living in distant places, closer to their native culture or community.

The resiliency of such developments lies in our recognizing that our happiness as individuals, and indeed our survivability as a species, depends on limiting our material consumption of food, energy, and resources to the minimum that we need in order to sustain ourselves physically, so that we can greatly expand the non-material wealth that lies latent in our midst, in the creative ideas, innovative insights, and inventive discoveries that everyone has something to contribute to and benefit from. In such a future, Thoreau's observation — "A man is rich in proportion to the number of things he can afford to let alone" — might become a motto that we all learn to live by and whose paradoxical truth we all come to realize, each in our own way.[8]

21

Fracture-Critical Buildings

When the 2010 earthquake in Haiti killed a couple of hundred thousand people in a matter of minutes, it revealed the suddenness with which fracture-critical structures—in this case, poorly reinforced and badly constructed buildings, and precariously sited and improperly secured hillside dwellings—can collapse and cause harm.[1] Many have viewed Haiti, the poorest country in the Western Hemisphere, as a special case in explaining the extent and severity of the damage, especially in the capital Port-au-Prince. But while the situation in Haiti may have exceeded the disasters of other countries in terms of lives lost per capita, we cannot ignore the message that that catastrophe has sent.

Many of the fastest-growing and most impoverished cities in the world, for example, stand on active seismic zones or in low-lying coastal areas subject to earthquakes or post-tremor tsunamis.[2] If we thought the recovery of Haiti has cost a lot of money—in the trillions of dollars—wait until a similar scenario occurs in a much larger city. But the same thinking and some of the same threats that caused the destruction in Haiti exists even in the most developed parts of the planet. We have still seen buildings and bridges crumble in California, for example, despite that state's strict seismic code, and there remain hazards, such as the likelihood of falling glass from skyscrapers or fires from broken gas and severed electrical lines, that can cause widespread injury or death in even the most modern city in the wake of an earthquake.[3] The real danger lies not in the physical harm these fracture-critical elements can cause in a quake, but the mental complacency that prevents us from acting on these threats, knowing their probability.

The design and engineering community has long known how to minimize the damage during earthquakes, ranging from more traditional methods like shear walls and cross-bracing to more exotic methods like base-isolated foundations and energy dissipating counterweights.[4] But the appearance of stability in buildings and the other structures we use on a daily basis, combined with a reluctance on the part of many people to think about the consequences of a major earthquake—or other equally powerful natural events like hurricanes, tsunamis, floods, and tornadoes—make it hard to get people to act to minimize the threat. Whether it comes from a lack of political will to mandate such precautions, a lack of money to incorporate such methods, or a lack of understanding about the risks involved, we continue to occupy a built environment full of preventable life-threatening risks.

Those same factors play into other often-overlooked aspects of our physical surroundings. The collapse of the World Trade Center Towers on September 11, 2001 exemplifies one aspect of this failure of imagination on our part. The buildings met the requirements of the building codes at the time, and their design addressed the typical forces that play upon such tall structures, including the possibility that the largest jet known at the time—a Boeing 707—could conceivably get lost in a fog and strike one of the towers.[5] No one, though, apparently anticipated the effect of an intense jet fuel fire, which led the buildings to collapse completely and remarkably quickly. The terrorists, in other words, took advantage of a vulnerability on our part: our tendency to see different and superficially unrelated systems in isolation from each other. The skyscraper represents one such system, the airline system another. And while both occupy the same airspace, especially in large cities like New York, we have assumed that we can keep these two systems from colliding into each other, without trying to imagine all of the scenarios in which they would. This is how fracture-critical design happens: from a failure to connect apparently disconnected things. Each system—the skyscraper and the airplane—may have multiple backups and redundancies to prevent a failure from occurring within the system itself, but by not accounting for the intersection of two seemingly separate systems—and not accounting for the diabolical inventiveness of people intent on doing harm—we made people unnecessarily vulnerable. As with infrastructure generally, the lack of resiliency among systems on a large scale can negate the resiliency of individual systems at a smaller scale.

This disconnect among related systems occurs at all scales, from systems the size of the airline system or modern skyscrapers, down to the scale of a house or the objects within it—the scale, in other words, that most of us have the capacity to address. Near my house stands a nineteenth-century wood-framed farmhouse—now part of a farm museum in the middle of the city—that has, in its front yard, the excavation of the structure that the farm family lived in when they first settled the land: a one-room, earth-sheltered, sod-roofed log cabin.[6] Given the relatively small dimensions of that cabin and the primitive water-proofing methods of the nineteenth century, the adjacent two-story, multi-roomed, clapboard-sided house, with its wrap-around porch, looks like progress, as it no doubt felt like to the family at the time. But knowing what we know now, does that still hold true today?

That farmhouse—and the twentieth-century suburban houses visible all around it—reflects the brute-force way in which we have responded to the diverse climates and contexts in which we live. Rather than adapt to the conditions in which we find ourselves and develop an appropriate architecture in response to them, we have, instead, adopted standard models that we build in warm regions as well as cold ones, in humid climates as well as arid ones. We then use technology, most of it fossil fueled, to make up for that lack of attention to our locales.

The consequences have become readily apparent: buildings consume about three-quarters of the electricity we consume and emit about half of all the greenhouse gases humans generate.[7] And while many of us have begun to try to change that by using more energy-saving appliances and equipment and by better insulating and weatherproofing houses, for example, our efforts have so far had a modest impact because of the fracture-critical nature of our houses themselves. Many of us in the United States live in houses larger than we really need and ill-suited to the climates in which we live. As a result, many of us remain dependent on a limited supply of increasingly expensive fuel sources to heat and cool large volumes of space with extensive amounts of surface area exposed to the weather. No amount of energy strategies will ever make our houses truly efficient as long as these buildings fight their location. However resilient our houses might be functionally or structurally, the lack of resiliency in our energy system and our over-dependence on a finite and fracture-critical fuel supply, makes all of us vulnerable, living in

Figure 21.1 Many of us in the U.S. live in houses larger than we really need and ill-suited to the climates in which we live. As a result, many of us remain dependent on a limited supply of increasingly expensive fossil fuels to condition large volumes of space with a lot of surface area exposed to the weather.

houses that would become uninhabitable at certain times of the year without heating or cooling.

I mention the site near my house not because I think we should all live in one-room, earth-sheltered structures. But as I stood at the excavation of that family's first abode and looked up at their subsequent farmhouse, I couldn't help but wonder what life would have been like had we continued to develop houses that fit their location rather than fight it. In the case of that nineteenth-century family, they might have learned something from the Native Americans who lived on their land and who the family continued to allow to live there long after the forests had become farm fields. Native cultures around the world have all evolved shelter in tune with their climates and the materials readily available to them. In the temperate climate of the middle of the North American continent—Turtle Island as some Native cultures called it—lightweight tepees served well in summer, with heavier bark or sod-covered structures in winter.[8] While primitive in one sense, their architecture also had a remarkable elegance and efficiency that might serve as a model or at least a metaphor for us, as we rediscover what our ancestors and those who preceded us on this land once knew.

Sustainability, in that sense, constitutes a profoundly conservative activity of relearning lessons of the past, when humans lived in greater harmony with the world, while envisioning a future different from the radically ill-suited one we have created since the mid-nineteenth century. Implicit in that is the idea that we have conflated conservatism and liberalism over the last century. Many modern "conservatives" echo eighteenth- and nineteenth-century liberalism, with its desire to protect individuals from oppressive government and its faith in minimally regulated markets. Likewise many modern "liberals" represent twentieth-century liberalism, with its belief in the benefits of government to help people and its conviction that markets need regulation in order to function properly.[9] Thus the political battles of our own time, between the party of big business or that of big government, have become tantamount to a family feud among liberals, all the more virulent perhaps because of the familial nature of the fight. This has become so much the norm that we rarely see the radical way of life that both political parties seek to protect, and that conservatives, historically, would have absolutely opposed. This suggests that the time has come for a new politics that doesn't argue, as many Republicans and Democrats now do, about different flavors of liberalism—the nineteenth- or twentieth-century versions—but that, instead, understands the reason why, for example, conservative and conservation spring from the same root word. Such a position would arise from a deep understanding and appreciation of how humans have lived in harmony on this planet for thousands of years, prior to the nineteenth century, and a belief that we need to embrace the principles behind a conservation-oriented conservatism if we want to live thousands more years.

Such a political position presents us with a perfect design problem. Design works through analogy and so the sustainable ways in which native people have lived on every continent becomes, if not a literal model, at least a figurative way in which we might once again inhabit the earth. The tepee, and similar structures native to a particular place, should serve as a metaphor for housing in our own time that sits lightly on the land and that lends itself to rapid deployment should circumstances require us to move.

That is no idle notion. At a time when climate change has begun to lead to increasingly severe weather conditions—extreme heat or cold, ever-more-powerful hurricanes and tornadoes, increasingly intense floods or droughts—the ability to move, or rather flee, may become a valuable feature of inhabitation. Meanwhile, the instability of earthquake-prone land and tsunami-prone seashores makes a lighter-weight and more mobile form of dwelling highly appealing, since it will not crush inhabitants should it collapse in a tremor or demand the fixed foundations that lead people to live in vulnerable locations, in harm's way.

As so often happens with design, though, the best response to a problem can challenge accepted ways of thinking, and the idea of a less permanent and more pliable form of housing comes up against the assumptions we often hold about property. Unlike many native people, who saw the land as belonging to the group and resulting from its collective stewardship, most nations have divided the land up into private property and granted its owners exclusive rights—a radical idea that has gotten turned on its head and become a "conservative" one. Whatever the arguments for or against property rights, the division of the land into private ownership comes at an enormous public cost, one that we all bear, for it implies that people have a right to live wherever they want and that the rest of us have a responsibility to help protect them from the hazards that might plague them there.

Such brute-force living, based on the idea that we can resist—or get compensated for—whatever forces nature might send our way, has begun to seem like a really bad idea in an era in which the number and severity of climate and seismic-related disasters have continually increased. When we look, instead, at how humans have lived for most our history, it forces us to rethink property not as something fixed, but instead as something that we take with us as conditions warrant. This, in turn, suggests that the land itself becomes not ours to own, use and exploit as we wish, but instead ours to protect for our use and that of our children and grand-children for generations to come. That isn't communism, it is conservation-minded conservatism at its best.

Designing for Durability

22

This does not mean that everything must become impermanent. Human societies have long made the distinction between temporary (and usually privately owned) buildings and enduring (and usually public) ones. The distinguishing feature of our own era lies in our having often forgotten or overlooked that distinction. We even, sometimes, invert that traditional relationship, with formerly impermanent and now lavishly built private homes and poorly constructed public buildings, which we used to build to last and now we put up with the lowest bidder. That confusion continues down to the smallest details of our habitat. Materials that can last a very long time often get assembled in ways that greatly reduce their longevity by being combined with much less durable materials, which determine how long the whole will last before being carted off to a landfill.

Given the advanced technology and remarkable materials we now have available to us, you would think that the buildings we inhabit would last a long time and provide unprecedented durability. But, at least in the United States, our tax structure and financial system offers little incentive to build to last. If anything, it assumes a rate of depreciation far faster than the lifetime of the structures and materials we typically use, which has several perverse consequences. It depresses research in the building sector, which remains at a very low level in comparison to other major areas of our economy; it discourages investments in quality materials and careful craftsmanship, evident in the relatively large amount of litigation related to construction problems; and it dissuades the development of assemblies, systems, and enclosures that can resist long-term use and exposure, visible in the peeling paint, stained materials, and deteriorating cladding so often seen in buildings.[1]

If anything, we tend to treat buildings a lot like we do other fracture-critical systems. Just as the New Orleans levees provided just one barrier between the water and the entire interior of the city, so many buildings have a single layer of protection between the elements and the interior of the structure, often in the form of caulk joints at critical junctures. When these fail, the resulting leaks can damage finishes, promote rot, and feed mold and mildew, which in turn can reduce the value of the building, undermine its structural stability, and harm the health of its inhabitants.[2] Why do we let that happen? As in so many of the fracture-critical systems we construct, the risk involved in failure does not appear to justify the increased cost of prevention.

We have been fooled by such appearances, however. The lack of durability and risk of deterioration in so many buildings reflects not only the rapid depreciation allowed by our tax system, but also the rapid rate at which many people have historically moved in the United States.[3] Too few of us, at least before the financial collapse, seemed to stay around long enough to worry about the leaks or rot or mold that might exist within walls or behind paint. It's as if, despite the emphasis some place on private property rights, we have already begun to act as a nomadic people, moving on when times get tough, while still wanting buildings that look solid and recall a time when people stayed in one place much longer than we do now.

This raises an issue too often overlooked when we talk about the built environment. We typically think of our houses and offices, factories and farms, schools and shops in terms of the cost, quantity, and quality of space they enclose, but in the future, we will need to value the structures we occupy more in terms of time than space. Time lies at the very core of what sustainability entails, evident in the word itself. Its root word, "sustain," is essentially a time-based idea: to sustain means "to keep going," "to bear or endure." And, as we have seen from native settlements and even from our own ancestors a couple of centuries or more ago, many pre-modern buildings embodied a time-based way of thinking.

Permanent buildings—temples, cathedrals, monuments, and the like—employed relatively permanent materials, such as masonry walls, stone floors, and vaulted roofs, in configurations of space that remained fairly constant, based on functions that changed very slowly. Such buildings resisted change and represented ideas of eternity. Meanwhile, most private buildings in such cultures, as we know from the archeological and anthropological evidence, disappeared with hardly a trace above ground, often using readily available materials that returned to the earth from which they came: bamboo or wood in tropical climates, sun-dried brick or rammed earth in arid ones, sod or snow in the arctic, timber and plaster in temperate zones. Like the cycles of the seasons, which served as the dominant metaphor for time in many pre-Modern cultures, buildings came and went, arose and decayed, with the fact of such cycles itself being the one constant.

In contrast, many Modern buildings have erased the difference between the temporary and the eternal or so mixed them up that they remain temporally incoherent. While the cycles of change in buildings have increased in frequency, as people move, offices change, and functions shift in a fast-paced modern world, we continue to develop materials that have ever-greater durability and longevity. We now have rot-resistant wood unaffected by contact with the ground, corrosion-resistant steel able to be exposed to the elements, and temperature-resistant concrete set in place any time of the year. But we place these ever-more durable materials in ever-more changeable situations, reflecting a seeming inability to distinguish between the permanent and impermanent. Why have rot-resistant wood adjoined to easily rotted sheathing or corrosion-resistant steel in buildings likely to be altered or demolished in a matter of decades?

Or take the typical wall in almost every building we build. We mix a permanent material—gypsum, capable of lasting thousands of years—with semi-permanent materials such as aluminum or wood, which last a long time if protected from water, and with relatively impermanent materials such as the paper facing on the gypsum board, which tears easily and mildews quickly in the presence of moisture. We then fasten all of these materials together into single assemblies, allowing the longevity of the least durable material to determine the timeframe of the whole.[4] We assume that such assemblies will last a long time if kept dry, but we also run plumbing in these walls, expect interior moisture to move through them, and depend on caulk joints to keep out exterior precipitation, countering the very logic of the system.

Even when we use masonry bearing walls, traditionally the most "permanent" assemblies, we often reduce their durability. In a masonry cavity wall, we typically connect durable materials—the brick cladding and a concrete block backup wall, for instance—with metal ties, vulnerable to corrosion. As if to aid that corrosion, we then provide outlets for water in the cavity to drain out of the wall, although mortar droppings frequently block the weep holes and cause water to back up in the cavity, which can lead the metal ties to rust and this supposedly permanent assembly to fall apart prematurely.

Meanwhile, we keep developing new products to address the symptoms of this planned obsolescence, such as coating the brick with a water-resistant sealer, which can exacerbate the moisture problems and accelerate the wall's deterioration by trapping water vapor in the cavity. We continue to tinker with building materials and assemblies in response to such problems. Every year, manufacturers come up with new products meant to correct some aspect of the way we build, to make it more efficient or less costly, but by not challenging the underlying flaw in the logic of so much modern construction, we end up squandering far more than we save. Our landfills are full to overflowing with materials that, given their inherent longevity and the amount of energy they embody, should not be there. And we have let this extraordinarily wasteful process go on for so long that, as already happens in developing countries, even developed nations may start "mining" landfills for once plentiful and now scarce materials in coming decades.

How, then, can we extend the life of buildings or decrease the longevity of their components or both, so that our use of buildings will last as long as their materials and our materials will last no longer than the usefulness of buildings? We can lay out spaces and dimension them in ways that allow for a diversity of future uses, far beyond the building's initial purpose. History offers us a plethora of examples of how to do this, with plan arrangements, room dimensions, and circulation patterns that lend themselves to the accommodation of multiple activities and a diversity of inhabitation. Some occupants who have a short time horizon in terms of their use of a building may not care about such adaptability and may even see it as a waste of time and money to provide it, but the real waste comes

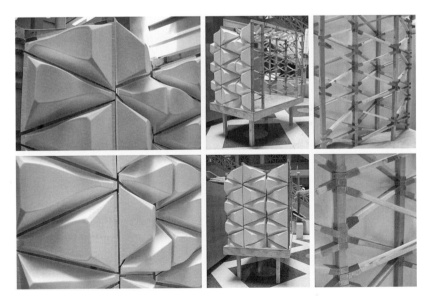

Figure 22.1 Too many of the buildings we construct are too expensive to build and too hard to recycle. HouMinn is one of many design firms exploring ways of using digital fabrication to speed construction, reduce its cost, and enable the reuse of materials. Images of the Oswall installation by HouMinn Practice at the University of Houston Green Building Components Exhibition.

with disposing of structures that still have a great deal of residual value.[5] Indeed, the shortsightedness of throwing away something still good underlies all fracture-critical thinking.

But if short-term gain and rapid write-offs remain public policy, we can take the opposite tack and focus on reducing the longevity of all but the most ceremonially significant buildings, the strategy most common among our ancestors. This involves making different choices in almost everything we use, employing rapidly biodegradable, easily recyclable, or highly renewable materials and products, and readily demountable, quickly dismantled, or simply rearranged assemblies and systems.

That, in turn, will require a change in our expectations, as we return to using mostly local materials, natural finishes, and lightweight or easily deconstructed assemblies like those in most vernacular buildings. This does not mean we will also return to living in traditional ways. A more resilient and responsible future will likely involve a combination of that older mindset with advanced technology, rapid communication, and greater knowledge of human needs and global ecologies.

23

Fracture-Critical Consumption

The confusion between the permanent and impermanent stems from a deeper confusion between needs and wants. The economist Manfred Max-Neef has outlined a useful way of thinking about that, arguing that all people, regardless of cultural differences, have basic needs in common that are readily identifiable, easily addressed, and relatively few in number. Max-Neef lists them as: subsistence, protection, affection, understanding, participation, recreation, creation, identity, and freedom. How we satisfy those needs, however, differs dramatically from one place or time to another. "What is culturally determined," he writes, "are not the fundamental human needs, but the satisfiers for those needs. Cultural change is, among other things, the consequence of dropping traditional satisfiers for the purpose of adopting new or different ones." [1]

He goes on to identify different kinds of satisfiers. "Synergistic" ones address more than one need simultaneously: public education, for example, involves understanding, participation, creation, and identity. "Singular" ones address only one need and no others: the game of solitaire might provide us recreation but little else. Meanwhile "inhibiting" ones address one need to the exclusion or destruction of others: governmental wire-tapping of its own citizens might increase protection from terrorists, but destroys our freedom. Max-Neef also points to the large number of what he calls "pseudo-satisfiers," things that appear to satisfy one or more need, but that

Figure 23.1 Consumer culture often gives us a false sense of choice. While the number and superficial variety of products can seem overwhelming, the amount of true diversity remains remarkably small and, especially in our food system, the number of products that are truly good for us is even smaller.

remain empty promises or that simply encourage us to seek more of the same.[2]

When we look across much of what our consumer culture produces, a huge amount of it consists of such pseudo-satisfiers. We have many products that promise one thing and deliver something else: cars that promise freedom, but end up making us dependent upon them; cigarettes that promise recreation, but end up causing disease; or radio talk shows that promise understanding, but end up instilling prejudice. Many other products give a kind of empty satisfaction: highly processed foods that may fill us up and seem to address our need for subsistence, but end up giving us very little nutrition; video games that may provide us with recreation, but end up making us more stressed; or advertising that may be catchy and even creative, but that always seems to make what it promotes seem better than it really is. Most of us tolerate these false forms of satisfaction as part of the background noise of our culture, but in a future of even greater environmental and cultural change, understanding Max-Neef's distinction between needs and wants will be critical, since we will have to become more creative in satisfying needs, given the limited resources we will have at our disposal.

Satisfiers that inhibit or destroy other needs or that turn out to be pseudo-satisfiers can hinder or harm not only people, but also the natural environment as well. Much of the enormous waste stream of paper, packaging, and throwaway products comes from pseudo-satisfiers, things that people bought or used and quickly discarded because they served no real need. At the same time, the energy used in manufacturing and shipping all of this material, which might be used once and end up sitting in a landfill for thousands of years, demands a great deal of the fossil fuels we burn.[3] The average American, for example, consumes over ten times the resources of a person in less-developed countries such as India or China, all because of the different ways these cultures have gone about satisfying the same needs.[4] Nor are "green" technologies necessarily better, for, while they can make things more environmentally friendly, the quantity of goods can remain so high and the quality of the satisfier so low that we can end up using almost as much energy and generating just as much waste as we did before we became "green." What we need to examine critically is a process that the critic Michael Ignatieff calls the "upward spiral of needs," in which luxuries in one generation or in one culture become necessities in another.[5] Caught up in this upward spiral, we start to lose sight of actual human need, and begin to think, instead, that what we need is the satisfiers that those around us have and that our grandparents would have considered luxuries.

Although offered for what seems like a worthy goal of maximizing our convenience, pleasure, and freedom of choice, the plethora of goods many of us have available to us can have the opposite effect of making it harder to decide what to choose and, paradoxically, making us less happy or satisfied as a result. As research on the subject has shown, happiness does not come from simply having more—more possessions, more choices—but from having more of what has meaning to us.[6] Also, beyond a certain point—a $75,000 annual income in the United States according to recent research—no additional amount of money makes us any happier, suggesting what seems like a reasonable cap on personal income in order to ensure as many people as possible make that benchmark.[7]

The sheer variety of options available to us may arise out of a good intent; given the diversity of people's interests, manufacturers and service providers often like to offer the greatest range of alternatives for people to choose from: I might like blue, you might like red, and so companies want to make sure their widgets are available in both. But are those meaningful differences? Haven't we, in the process, created a system in which we have a seemingly infinite number of superficial choices with very few fundamental ones? We may have all sorts of options in terms of what we can get in a new car, but in most American cities, at least, if we don't have an automobile we have very few other options of getting around: a lot of choices and no real choice at all.

By confusing needs and wants, and by putting so much of our energy and effort into producing and consuming pseudo-satisfiers, we have completely forgotten the very idea behind the word "economy" – doing the most with the least: the least cost, the least waste, and so on. Adam Smith, a philosophy professor, would have completely understood and appreciated the distinction that Max-Neef makes and would, I believe, view the current over-consumption of resources by a few and the ongoing poverty of a great many as capitalism gone awry.

A form of capitalism closer to what the word "economy" actually means would result in a happier and more satisfying capitalism, to use Max-Neef's term. It would also stop many in the modern world from over-consuming, to the detriment of themselves and their progeny, and extend the invisible hand of the market to meet the synergistic needs of all people. That may sound contrary to capitalism, but not so. As a stoic, Smith set up a system that would enable us not only to thrive, but also to handle the unexpected setbacks – and designed disasters – that have plagued us.[8] So what would such a capitalism, a truer form of it, look like?

24

Creative Citizen Consumption

To answer that question, we might find it helpful to reframe Max-Neef's insights in terms of design. Design serves human needs, but it also helps fuel our desires, resulting in our sometimes wanting what we don't really need and needing what we didn't know we wanted. This seems paradoxical enough at the scale of the individual. At the scale of hundreds of millions and soon billions of people pursuing the over-consuming behavior of the wealthiest countries, that paradox becomes almost dangerous, as ever-more people want goods they can live without, exhausting resources, extinguishing species, and threatening our very existence in the process.

We have, in essence, inverted psychologist Abraham Maslow's hierarchy of needs. He depicted human needs in terms of a pyramid, with the satisfaction of physiological needs (food, clothing, shelter, sex) and safety needs (the security of one's self, family, and property) as essential before we can satisfy the higher-order needs of love (friendship, family), esteem (respect of and by others), and self-actualization (creativity, spontaneity, and problem solving).[1]

In the pursuit of a seemingly endless supply of products to meet our need for self-actualization, we have neglected our physiological and safety needs, with too many poor people across the planet lacking adequate food, safe shelter, or personal security, and too many of the rich impoverished with the over-consumption of pseudo-satisfiers, as Max-Neef would say.

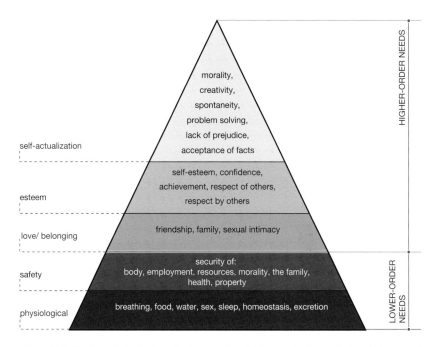

Figure 24.1 Abraham Maslow's hierarchy of needs. If we think of our fracture-critical world in terms of Abraham Maslow's hierarchy of needs, the physiological and safety needs of too many people remain unmet, with inadequate food, shelter, and personal security, even as the world's wealthiest impoverish themselves with the over-consumption of pseudo-satisfiers.

It's hard to feel sorry for the over-consumers, given the hundreds of millions of people who have little access to clean water, reliable sanitation, and safe housing. Too many lack even the most fundamental physiological needs, and no amount of outside aid seems able to keep up with the ever-growing number of unmet needs. By turning Maslow's hierarchy upside down and focusing so much money and energy on the self-actualization of the few, the physiological needs of all remain unmet.

Design helps drive, at least in part, that inversion of needs. When we focus on the newest model, the latest trend, and the hippest style, designed objects and environments contribute to the sense of unquenched desires, even as our needs go unmet. But if design remains part of the problem, how might it become, instead, a part of the solution? How might design contribute to the right-siding of Maslow's pyramid of needs and to the satisfying of basic requirements so that as many as possible might someday find love, esteem, and self-actualization?

The citizen consumer movement offers one answer.[2] Green design, eco-friendly products, and socially responsible activities have emerged in recent years in response to the growing concern about the harmful effects on others of our individual consumer decisions. In contrast to the conspicuous consumption of past eras, citizen consumption involves reusing existing products, repurposing what others discard, and recycling what we don't absolutely need. And with that sense of our being citizens before being consumers has come a design aesthetic that makes a virtue of the unexpected, the fortuitous, and the ad hoc, reveling in what we have at hand rather than obsessing about what we do not have.

The ethically driven aesthetic of the citizen consumer movement represents a profound shift in thinking from the last century. Too often, in the past, we have separated ethics and aesthetics, with those focused on the latter finding those interested in the former to be boring, blinkered, or blind to the beauty of the world.[3] Citizen consumption, though, represents a refusal to dichotomize these two closely related human goals. It recognizes the inherent relationship of the good and the beautiful and it dismisses the easy cynicism of post-modernism, which became, perhaps too cynically, the hand-maiden of our global over-consumption. Denying the connection between the good and the beautiful, between ethics and aesthetics, simply enabled those who did not want to face up to the lack of ethics to emphasize, instead, the independence of aesthetics and in so doing to sugar coat otherwise objectionable actions.

This did not happen in all cases, but it happened enough to make the rejoining of ethics and aesthetics a major first step in refocusing us on what most needs our attention: not the wealthy few, but the vast array of impoverished people and disappearing species. Aesthetics may seem far removed from the latter: why should we care what things look like as people starve and plants and animals face extinction? The reason lies in what aesthetics can do to advance an ethical goal. Ethics may convince us to act in a responsible and empathetic way toward others, but aesthetics gives us the emotional incentive to do so. If desire has driven us to over-consume things in ways good neither for us nor the planet, then we will need the desire to go in the opposite direction: to desire what we most need and to see the ultimate pointlessness in what we most want but do not need and cannot afford economically or environmentally.

That citizen-consumer aesthetic will likely look like what the energy intensive, materially wasteful world of the past did not. It will have a hand-made rather than a high-tech look, a do-it-yourself rather than a mass-produced quality, and a resourceful rather than a wasteful character. Such an aesthetic does, of course, exist among the myriad options we have as over-consumers of the world's resources. What will likely change, though, is the nature of options available to us. Consumer choice will come less from the manipulations of mass-produced products and the embellishments of one-off environments, and more from the creative responses of individuals and groups to their immediate situation, while fitting the materials they have at hand to their particular needs. This will greatly increase the choices we have to make, but greatly decrease the choices others make for us. Citizen consumption involves the active participation and co-creativity of the user and the designer, as opposed to people passively purchasing stuff, determined and dangled before us by design.

The shift from a consumer to a creator economy will also alter the role of the designer, who will become more of a facilitator and enabler and less of a promoter and procurer. That shift will also change the nature of peoples' consumption patterns, making us all more actively engaged in meeting our needs and creating the world around us, as humans have done for most of our history, as opposed to the last 150 years or so. This does not mean that we will return to a pre-nineteenth century, pre-modern condition. If anything, aesthetics will probably become as localized and as diverse as the people involved in its creation. And design, as the making of things people use, will likely become, once again, a central aspect of what people learn as part of doing what we need to do to survive—and thrive—in the world.

That process of local production and creative consumption may take longer than the typical project of today, but it can also generate a greater amount of collective wealth and community cohesion, more social capital even as it requires less financial capital. Likewise, that process may not produce results that meet the aesthetic expectations of critical elites who control our cultural capital. But the ethical grounding of this work fosters a different and equally valid form of cultural value. We may find this socially oriented consumption harder to measure than that driven by economic or cultural capital, but it has greater reach, since it can affect not just an individual but an entire community through the social bonds that a participatory, co-creative design process can engender.

Such a participatory practice may sound radical, but it is also a profoundly conservative practice in the sense of it being, by far, the oldest form of design production. Throughout most of human history, prior to the modern era, designers were themselves a part of the community in which they worked, acting largely anonymously, using mostly locally available materials and well-established methods, and serving mainly as the facilitators and interpreters of what a local community needed. Because we tend to view the past in terms of what matters most to us in the present, we typically see the history of design as being composed of the monuments and icons of economic power and cultural elites. With a different lens, that of social capital, we can see a very different history, in which indigenous or vernacular design as being represented the collective interests and efforts of communities of people over long periods of time, building social cohesion along with the physical structures that people erected for themselves.

Given the growing gaps between rich and poor around the globe, and the greatest inequity in the United States since the census started to collect such data, we have depended for too long on financial capital and cultural capital as the measure of wealth. And given the retrenchments and readjustments that will inevitably arise as a result of such inequities and imbalances, social capital will become increasingly important as people return to the one resource on which they can count: the mutual support systems of family and friends, neighbors, and community members. Participatory design, community production, and citizen consumption can help such social capital accrue. And with that accrual will come the resilience that we will all need when our fracture-critical consumer culture finally collapses under its own unsustainable and unsupportable weight.

PART III

Designing to Avoid Future Disasters

25

Why We Have So Much Bad Design

In a recent paper, economists Itzhak Ben-David, John R. Graham, and Harvey R. Campbell report on research that they conducted into chief financial officers in major American corporations, finding that most do not do a very good job at forecasting their financial future.[1] Maybe we should not expect this of them: who can predict with any accuracy something as complex as global finance, affected by so many unpredictable events? But the disturbing aspect of Ben-David, Graham, and Campbell's research lies in the seeming over-confidence that the CFOs expressed about their ability to make such predictions. CFOs think they are much better at this than they really are, suggesting that people in positions of power often think that the success of the entities they lead stems from their own genius, a hubris that can lead to their undoing. As economist Richard Thaler observed, "One route to the corner office is to combine over-confidence with luck, which can be hard to distinguish from skill."[2]

This pertains directly to the problem of bad design and suggests at least one reason why we have so much of it. An overconfident client or leader can make design itself seem irrelevant. One of the core skills of designers lies in the rigorous, iterative, and often punishingly critical process of envisioning possible futures. That often involves something very specific—a future building, product, or service, for example—but behind the instrumental goal of design-ing something that doesn't yet exist there lies a method of studying and critically evaluating a number of scenarios until the option that meets the greatest number of needs with the fewest possible problems eventually emerges. The public often doesn't see design—or creative activity generally—in this way. The popular image of creative genius, coming up with a brilliant idea like a bolt of lightning, completely misrepresents the long hours, repeated study, and constant revisions that almost always precede a good design, one that meets the stated needs within the given constraints.

Overconfident leaders and managers—like overconfident designers—may have bought into that popular culture image of the genius. Understandably, they can come to believe in their invincibility because of their prior success, and can become impatient with those who caution against making decisions too hastily or moving forward with too little study of the possible negative results or unintended consequences of an action. Good designers know all too well what can happen when impatience or intemperance leads to shortcuts in either the timeline of a design or in its execution. And, given the number of spectacularly expensive and damaging catastrophes we have experienced in recent years, the general public now knows as well. As business analyst Stuart Albert has observed, the timing of decisions can make all the difference between success and failure of an enterprise, and just as too much caution can lead to missed opportunities, so too little caution, without sufficient analysis of potential failure, can lead to even more calamitous losses.[3]

To avoid such disasters from happening, and to ensure that we don't inadvertently design our way into them again, we need a broader sense of what we mean by the word "design." The word has its origin in the Latin word "designo," which means to make a mark, to sketch, delineate, or trace out, as well as to signify, contrive, arrange, and regulate. In other words, design involves a range of human activities involving planning, organizing, and envisioning something that doesn't yet exist. The generality of the origin of the word "design" matters, for it can help us sketch a different future from what we have had in the past, one that will enable us to do a better job at sustaining ourselves.

We typically think of design in a much narrower way, mainly in terms of the products we buy—cars, computers, cameras—and the environments in which we spend most of our time—our homes and offices, stores and schools. Underlying almost everything we employ in our daily lives, from the attire we wear to the furniture we use to the fixtures we operate, design obviously plays a key role in economic activity; without design, many companies would have little to sell, and most people would have little to buy.

We rarely apply the word "design," however, to non-physical things, to systems, organizations, operations, conceptions, and methods. Indeed, when it comes to the system that overrides almost everything else humans do—the economy—many people remain openly hostile to the idea of design. The very term—a designed economy—may remind many of socialism, communism, or worse of something government bureaucrats do in totalitarian countries. That gets at the sometimes malevolent aspect of the word "design," in the sense of having "designs on someone," perpetrating something unwillingly on others.

Most of us think of the free-market economy as unplanned or undesigned, as individuals and organizations making economic decisions based on supply and demand, with prices that continually reset the balance between the two. At a conceptual level, that view of economics may hold true, but it overlooks, at a finer grain, the myriad ways in which design permeates our economy—and every economy. When Adam Smith wrote about the "invisible hand" of the market-place, he did not conceive of that hand as acting randomly or without intention. If anything, the marketplace remains full of people with "designs" on how to maximize returns on and minimize risks of investments. The issue has to do not with design per se, but with the way in which design occurs, top down or bottom up, based on the decisions of a few or of many.

That issue of top-down versus bottom-up design remains a key point of debate in the design community, and it underscores one of the primary reasons why we have designed our way into so many disasters. Because of the hostility in the past to the very idea of design, especially in our economy, we have ended up falling prey to global economic recessions and personal financial catastrophes that we could—and should—have avoided. Instead, the common misreading of the invisible hand of the marketplace makes too many of us too fatalistic about our ability to design an economic system—and the myriad systems that result from it—in ways that do not leave so many people, communities, and species so vulnerable to the designs that a relatively few people, investment bankers as much as government bureaucrats, have had on us.

The real problem lies not with design itself, but with the inept way in which design has occurred in parts of our economy that many people don't think of as designed. If ineptitude sounds like a strong word, consider this: what would we call it if a company offered products that not only harmed many of its customers, but the very people who designed and marketed those products, who had such a poor understanding of what they created that it brought their entire company down? Assuming such self-destructive behavior did not represent intentional malice, the only other explanation has to involve some combination of incredible ignorance and gross incompetence. And yet, because we don't think of financial products in the same that we think of cars, computers, or cell phones, we don't see what happened to investment banks like Bear Sterns and Lehman Brothers as a profound design failure that needs the same kind of regulation and oversight that we insist on in the auto or electronics industries in order to protect consumers—and the companies themselves. The Dodd-Frank Wall Street Reform Act is a long-overdue effort in that direction.[4]

Product designers spend years preparing to do this work, gaining a lot of skill and experience in the process. And despite the popular misconception that design involves mainly talent and intuition that either you have or you do not, the activity that generates almost everything we use in our daily lives demands a great deal of discipline. So why do we entrust the design of other kinds of products to those who often have never taken so much as one course in design? That may have something to do with the paradoxical nature of design, which is its pervasiveness and its simultaneous invisibility. Like the very air we breathe, the designed world we occupy seems always with us, and because of that most people remain largely unaware of the work that goes into creating everything we use and occupy in our daily lives. The invisibility of design has also affected designers in some respects. The design disciplines have long accepted the idea that they create physical things, while overlooking the fact that the systems, services, and structures that we depend on in the process of living our lives have been designed as well.

Think about what we do when we go shopping. We go to a store or go online and get a cart, we find the goods we want in locations organized in some logical and legible way, and we then proceed to a cash register in order to pay. Throughout that process, we interact not just with the products we seek, which someone designed, packaged, and marketed, but also with the systems devised to make our ability to shop even possible: the system of putting products in particular places so that we can find them most easily, the system of cashiers — virtual or real — that enables us to make the transaction quickly and conveniently, and the system of banks and other lending institutions that allow us to pay with cash, check, or credit or debit card. Add to that the system of ordering, transporting, storing, and stocking goods in the store; the system of hiring, paying, and supervising the people who work in the store; the system of heating, cooling, and lighting that makes the store — at least the physical version — inhabitable; and the system of building and zoning ordinances that enables shoppers to find and access the store and that ensures their safety inside, and you quickly see the store not just as a designed enclosure for designed goods, but also as part of designed systems that operate at a range of scales, each adjusted to its purpose.

In some ways, design may experience in the twenty-first century what science did in the twentieth century—what science writer Richard Panek has called its "invisible century."[5] Panek writes about how some scientists at the end of the nineteenth century thought that science had largely understood everything about the physical world, and that science, as they understood it, had come to an end. Little did they know that, with the coming of the twentieth century, science would discover the "invisible" world, with Freud's exploration of the subconscious, Einstein's theories of relativity, and Max Plank's descriptions of quarks among many discoveries, including the human genome effort in the latter part of the century. The "invisible" world has become as central to scientific inquiry as the visible one.

Design stands at the brink of a similar "invisible century." While designers will continue to create the products and environments that we use and inhabit in our daily lives, the design community has begun to discover that the demand for how we think is as great in the invisible world of systems, policies, procedures, and processes. Designing a less vulnerable financial system, a less error-prone healthcare system, a less convoluted policy arena, and a less polarized political process are among the most important areas that designers can help with. Designers have the training to look for system failures, to investigate possible solutions, to explore analogies from other fields, to prototype and test new procedures, and to find the simplest way of achieving the best results—all of which would benefit the invisible designed world that has increasingly failed us.

Not that what we design never fails. Despite a design process that has evolved to catch possible failures before they are enacted, unintended errors still, on occasion, do occur. In fact, designers have developed failure as a central part of their process. The discipline of design involves the iterative activity of developing ideas, prototyping, testing and critiquing them, refining them, and starting over again until the best ideas emerge, fully developed, to meet the greatest number of needs in the most elegant and cost-effective manner. But the disasters we increasingly face come from areas of our economy and society not often thought of as designed, not created with designers as part of their development, and so not well designed, with the possibility of failure in mind. The answer does not entail putting some bureaucrat in some central government office to turn the levers of industry; that image of the demonic, dictatorial designer has become so out-dated and irrelevant that we should not even waste our time thinking about it. Instead, the way to avert disasters in the future entails seeing them mostly as the result of design failures and starting to engage designers not just in the creation of sellable products or rentable space, but also in the very conception and critique of the systems, services, and structures we all depend on and suffer from should they fail.

This aligns completely with a free-market economy. As business school dean, Roger Martin, has written:

> Businesspeople don't just need to understand designers better—they need to become designers . . . For any company that chooses to innovate, the foremost challenge is this: Are you willing to step back and ask, "What's the problem we're trying to solve?" Well, that's what designers do: They take on a mystery, some abstract challenge, and they try to create a solution . . . In the end, design is about shaping a context, rather than taking it as it is. When it comes to design, success arises not by emulating others, but by using organizational assets and integrative thinking to identify, build on, and leverage asymmetries, evolving unique models, products and experiences—in short, creative business solutions.[6]

Nor does Martin stand alone in advocating for a new role for designers in our economy. As the writer Daniel Pink has asked in his popular book, *A Whole New Mind*:

> What if we could identify companies that have integrated design into their very business model? Would they make good investments? . . . The answer is a resounding yes . . . Five publicly-held companies that differentiate based on design: Apple, Target, Starbucks, Motorola, and Procter & Gamble . . . have easily outperformed the S&P 500 and the NASDAQ over the last five years . . . Maybe it's time for an index of companies that grasp this new competitive logic of business. Call it the DADI, for Design as Differentiator Index.[7]

Were we to have such an index we might find what researchers in the UK discovered—that, on average, design-alert businesses have increased their market share by 6.3 percent over companies that are not design savvy, with those in the retail sector increasing their share by 6.9 percent. Less than half of design-alert businesses compete mainly on price compared to two-thirds of those who don't use design, and shares in design-led businesses have outperformed the top 100 companies on the London stock exchange by more than 200 percent over the past decade.[8]

We live in a designed world, with an economy increasingly design based and design dependent, and yet we have yet to integrate design thinking into especially the invisible systems, non-tangible services, and ephemeral products that have taken an ever-larger share of economic activity. Until we make that transition to the "whole new mind" Pink talks about, we will have to endure the consequences of failed banking systems, toxic financial products, unmarketable real-estate assets, over-extended infrastructure, and unsustainable industries — all disasters waiting to happen. What is that design mind like, and how can we begin to employ it to stem the tide of catastrophes that has resulted from so many years of bad design?

26

The Design Mind

We all have the capability of designing. Like any number of other basic capabilities — music, speech, writing, mathematical calculation, and so on — design remains fundamental to human beings. When we put on a particular combination of clothing in the morning, look ahead to the day and plan accordingly, arrange a variety of things into a greater whole, solve problems that we have not encountered before, act on a hunch without clear evidence to back up our intuition, see connections among things that seem otherwise unrelated, and play out scenarios about events in the future — all of those activities involve our thinking and acting in a designed way. Design involves purpose and function, but it also engages a part of our mind that can see something that doesn't yet exist, and so it remains one of the key skills we have in shaping the world around us according to some intention or goal.

Because we live in a world that tends to recognize extremes and to downplay the things we have in common, most of us don't think of ourselves as designers. We generally reserve that for people trained as such or for people who have a gift in that area, for someone who has design talent outside the norm. As a result, we often don't think of what we all do on a daily basis as involving design. Likewise, we often don't see how much design pervades our lives. We absolutely depend on it in order to function and we cannot escape it, however much we might try. Just look around. Virtually everything you see has

Figure 26.1 We have deskilled most of the human population by overly professionalizing activities that people used to know how to do. Professionals can build resilience back into communities by becoming better communicators, facilitators, and advisors rather than experts with some sort of mysterious and unassailable knowledge.

been designed: the room that surrounds you and the chair you occupy, the building you work or live in and the clothing you wear, the book or electronic device in front of you and the roads, vehicles, landscape, and infrastructure outside the nearby window. Design is "making things better for people," as the designer Richard Seymour put it, knowing that, as designer Bill Moggridge quipped, "a lot of trial and error goes into making things look effortless."[1]

Because of the pervasiveness of our designed surrounding, we rarely think about it. Like fish in water, we swim in a sea of design and so take it for granted that we don't know how much it affects us or how much we each engage in it. The invisibility of design occurs especially—and ironically—when done well. Peter Senge, of MIT's Sloan School of Management, has observed that "The functions of design . . . are rarely visible; they take place behind the scenes. The consequences that appear today are the result of work done long in the past, and work today will show its benefits far in the future."[2] We usually become aware of design when done badly, when something designed inconveniences us, makes us uncomfortable, or fails in such a way that it harms us or results in a great deal of damage.

We have sought to protect ourselves from bad design by professionalizing its creation. Having done so with other fields that affect our health, safety, and welfare, we hold designers responsible for their failures. While good as far as that goes, the problem lies in the fact that, as have seen, many non-designers, people who don't even know they do design, end up doing a lot of bad design, causing great harm, and producing the most massive failures — often unintentionally. We need professionally trained designers, but we also need a degree of understanding about design in the general population, at least enough so that people know what they don't know and where they can go to get help. In that sense, design, which involves the health of our physical environment, needs to become like human health, something that almost everyone knows enough about to recognize what they don't know and where to go to get the professional attention they need.

That also demands that professional designers rethink their roles. As we move into a much more complex and overcrowded world, the needs far outstrip the ability of professionally trained people to respond adequately. Accordingly, professionals need to become not just technical experts, but also facilitators of others who, to varying degrees, can guide and counsel people who have need of such advice but not the means for or access to it. I teach in a design college, where we educate our students to become designers — landscape architects and urban designers, architects and interior designers, apparel and graphic designers. They learn not only a number of technical skills and detailed knowledge, but also a way of thinking and a process of creating the designed products and environments we all use everyday. They work hard and their education takes years. We can only prepare a relatively few people, however, and as we have professionalized the field, design has mainly become available to a relatively small and very wealthy percentage of the world's population who can afford the fees.

To exacerbate the problem of a limited number of professional designers, the design community has chosen to operate according to a medical model of practice, in which professionals work with individual clients to address their particular needs. While that remains an important activity, key to the creation of much what we

Figure 26.2 Just as medicine gave birth to public health to attend to the health needs of those who could not directly pay for services, the design fields need a public health version of themselves, making the results of this value-creating activity available to all.

use in our lives, it leaves out the vast majority of the world's population that has a great need for design creativity—most valuable
when doing the most with the least—and who have little or no access
to designers. Design is perhaps the greatest social art, affecting the
most people of all the arts every day. That widespread effect suggests
that designers might consider, as an alternative form of practice, the
rise of the public health profession out of the medical field in the
nineteenth century, and give birth to a public-health version of
themselves. Design as a form of public health would enable us to
meet the needs of literally billions of people through affordable,
prototypical, and locally appropriate solutions to people's most
important physical problems. This new field would also help people
relearn how to design their world themselves, something that
humans all knew how to do before we turned to professionals to do
it for us.

While there remain important roles for professional designers, there also exists in everyone, to varying degrees, an ability to design. Unlike human activities that primarily utilize the left brain — math and language, for instance — or primarily use the right brain — art and music — design involves moving back and forth between the two hemispheres of our brains. Demanding both the analytical left brain and creative right brain, design engages in an iterative, cyclical process, involving the kind of practical creativity that not only produces the things we need in order to live, but also the innovations essential to success in a highly competitive global economy. Most of us think of designers as imaginative non-conformists, but what differentiates designers from, say, fine artists, lies in the strong left-brain logic that complements the right-brain creativity. Designers, in the end, make practical things: products, environments, systems, and structures that work, ideally beautifully, efficiently, and cost effectively. Learning how to design does not just equip us to create useful things, design also provides us with the sense of pleasure and accomplishment that comes from the process of doing so.

Many universities, of course, have design programs, but these creative fields often do not have the stature of the sciences. This reflects a larger problem in modern intellectual life: we have become exceptional in our ability to understand and explain the world as it exists, as science does with extraordinary amounts of data to make its case. We have not done nearly as good a job, however, in knowing what we should do differently in the future, based on that know-ledge. Many reasons for that probably exist. We don't have data about the future and so cannot back up our recommendations in the same way that we can through scientific analysis. Also, such recom-mendations can seem subjective, which objectively minded people often want to avoid, or seem politically charged, which publicly supported and donor-supported institutions may also want to avoid. The somewhat marginal role design plays in most universities reflects this dilemma: the discipline most capable of helping us imagine alternative futures remains somewhat marginalized in institutions charged with helping create a better world. As Adelle

Wapnick, founding director of advertising agency Cross Colours, observes, "Design is . . . an all-pervasive discipline that underpins almost everything we do, inhabit, eat, consume or adorn. More importantly, it's probably the most underestimated discipline in business."[3]

Part of the neglect of design in universities comes from its neglect in primary and secondary education. Although key to economic success, design almost never gets taught in preK–12 schools, and even when it does, it often gets lumped in with primarily right-brain subjects like fine art and music, fields that, unwisely, get cut during budget shortfalls. That neglect of the creative fields, as the writer Daniel Pink has argued, puts us at a great disadvantage in a world that increasingly needs the kind of right-and-left-brain thinking, the practical imagination that designers do. Indeed, our not seeing design thinking as a basic skill of all students may amount to one of the most competitively disadvantageous aspects of American education today.

As a result of this unfamiliarity with or suppression of design, we often equate it, wrongly, with aesthetics. The writer Bill Breen recognizes that "Design's power runs far deeper than aesthetics . . . If you are mapping out a sales strategy, or streamlining a manufacturing operation, or crafting a new system for innovating you are engaged in the practice of design."[4] Or we think, also wrongly, of design as simply about craft, about making things. "If business and design are to come together fruitfully on a large scale," says Patrick Whitney, director of the Institute of Design at IIT, ". . . change must come from separating design thinking from 'the crafting of things'. The power of design thinking must be freed up to deal with all sorts of issues on a global scale."[5]

What design really does is help us think in innovative, out-of-the-box ways, seeing the world as not just the result of logical, rational decision-making, but also as an emotional and deeply cultural response to reality that has a lot to do with the look and feel of things. Bruce Nussbaum of *Business Week* has shown how "Designers are teaching CEOs and managers how to innovate . . . They pitch themselves to businesses as a resource to help with a broad array of issues that affect strategy and organization—creating new brands, defining customer experiences, understanding user needs, changing business practices."[6] For that reason, it has become critical that we see design not as something that just goes on in the design department in a company, any more than we would see writing as only going on in the communications department or math only in the accounting department. "Design is the philosophical core of the company," writes John Zapolski of the Management Innovation Group. "Everyone in the company becomes involved in designing, whether that means creating financial plans or selecting casing materials for an industrial product. Design isn't something that the design department does. It's a way of operating the company. It's an ongoing set of choices about how the company is going to exist, to compete, to grow."[7]

Smart businesses and communities understand this, turning to what former Herman Miller president Ed Simon calls "organizational architects." "We need a new generation of organizational architects," says Simon. "But to get there we must first correct basic misunderstandings about the nature of business design. It's not just rearranging the organization structure. We have to get away from the P&L statement and design for the long term—based on understanding interdependencies. Most changes in organization structure are piecemeal reactions to problems. Real designers are continually trying to understand wholes."[8] And we don't just need people thinking like designers. We also need people skilled at managing the creative process of design, something only now being discussed in business schools. As Angela Dumas and Henry Mintzberg write, "This role of manager as designer is hardly mentioned in the literature, and barely acknowledged in business practice . . . Managers practice 'silent design' . . . the many decisions taken by non-designers who enter directly into the design process, no matter how unaware they or others may be of their impact."[9]

For all there are practical reasons for elevating design thinking, there also exist profound intellectual and cultural reasons for doing so. Design can change how we see ourselves in relation to each other and to the world around us, for design seeks to avoid win–lose situations and provide win–win solutions. As such, it involves less competition than collaboration, while helping us see the world not in terms of the survival of the fittest so much as an interdependent web of interactions to which we all contribute and upon which we all depend. As psychologist Rudi Webster puts it, "All stakeholders need to abandon their adversarial thinking and approach and engage in design thinking to find a win/win solution . . . It is simply about changing beliefs and perspectives and designing an optimal solution. Remember, it is beliefs that determine the limits of your achievements."[10]

27

The Process of Design

How can design help us create a better future for ourselves? Answering that question has taken on a certain urgency; it is something that we need to do if we are to thrive in the future. As psychologist Richard Farson, director of the Western Behavioral Sciences Institute, wrote at the opening of the twenty-first century:

> We will either design our way through the deadly challenges of this century, or we won't make it. For our institutions — in truth, for our civilization — to survive and prosper, we must solve extremely complex problems and cope with many bewildering dilemmas. We cannot assume that, following our present path, we will simply evolve toward a better world. But we can design that better world. That is why designers need to become leaders, and why leaders need to become designers.[1]

To design a better world, we need to understand the process that makes design as rigorous a discipline as any of the sciences, social sciences, or humanities. The popular media typically depicts designers, like those in other creative fields, as having bursts of insight that come suddenly and fully formed. While such sudden connections do occur in the design process, that process also involves a great deal of effort. The 10 percent inspiration/90 percent perspiration rule applies here; design occurs in a loopy way, in which the designer makes a move, critiques its flaws, and often takes a slight step back to reassess the idea in order to move forward in a more effective way. That two-steps-ahead-and-one-step-back process may seem frustrating to those of us who, educated in more left-brain ways, tend to see the world in more linear ways and success in terms of how quickly we get to a solution. But because design deals with what doesn't yet exist, it remains a process of probing into the future, creating it as we go. As computer scientist Herbert Simon wrote about design, it concerns itself "not with the necessary but with the contingent — not with how things are but with how they might be."[2]

Design shares with science and math the drive to understand the world, but it differs from them in a fundamental way. Most other disciplines try to comprehend the world as it is, dealing with the past and present; design remains one of the few fields that primarily tries to envision the world as it could be. To do this, designers often use analogies and metaphors to imagine what hasn't happened yet by likening it to what we know from the past and present. As Jeanne Liedtka of the University of Virginia's Darden School of Business puts it:

The most fundamental difference between [design and science] is that design thinking deals primarily with what does not yet exist; while scientists deal with explaining what is. That scientists discover the laws that govern today's reality, while designers invent a different future is a common theme. Thus, while both methods of thinking are hypothesis-driven, the design hypothesis differs from the scientific hypothesis.[3]

Designers, of course, engage in analysis, just as scientists and mathematicians do. Every time a designer draws general conclusions about a project from the specific needs in a client's program, or applies an overall theory of design to a particular project, induction and deduction occur. But design thinking has a "both–and" character and it involves reason and imagination in an almost continuous and near simultaneous flow. This, in turn, runs counter to the way most people have thought about thought itself, heavily influenced by Aristotle's "the law of the excluded middle," which holds that something cannot be one thing and something else at the same time.[4] Designers do not just take things apart and keep them distinct; we also put them back together and reconnect them in new ways, while accepting a high degree of ambiguity and simultaneity in the process. Designers also project ideas forward in time and space, toward unimagined possibilities. Designers, of course, also look to the past, to history for lessons and ideas, and to the present, to the sciences and social sciences for information and data. The distinguishing characteristic of design thinking, however, involves imagining the future, while accepting the fact that we can never know for certain what doesn't yet exist, in an iterative process that expands outward in order to focus in and takes steps backward in order to move forward to the best solution.

Certainty was served as the holy grail of modern thought, with science becoming the standard against which we measured other disciplines, and so the inherent fluidity and uncertainty of design made it seem undisciplined as a result. But with post-modern thought has come a much greater openness to ambiguity, complexity, and both–and solutions, which design excels at. While it remains to

Figure 27.1 As the psychologist Richard Farson has observed in his book *The Power of Design: A Force for Transforming Everything*, the complexity of the challenges we face requires a new field, which he calls "metadesign," that addresses the serious design flaws in the social, economic, and political systems that we depend on.

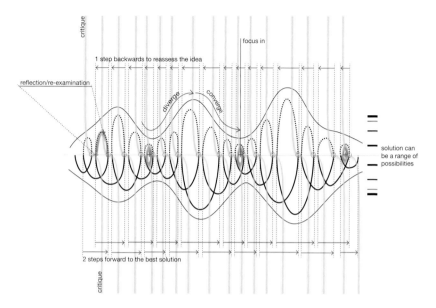

Figure 27.2 In a world increasingly viewed as a web rather than as a series of hierarchical silos, design thinking becomes especially valuable because of its ability to see the connections among disparate things, to navigate ambiguity in order to achieve results, and to envision alternative futures different from what we have known.

be seen how much designers can change the discipline's still somewhat marginal place in most universities, organizations, and corporations, it seems beyond a doubt that design thinking will need to become more central to intellectual life because of its ability to keep many seemingly contradictory ideas in play at the same time as a way of finding the most creative solutions.

Another aspect of design that distinguishes it from many other forms of thought involves its interweaving of thinking and making. Western thought has had a long-held suspicion of those who work with their hands, perhaps a reflection of the fact that the first academy that Plato founded in ancient Greece arose out of an aristocratic culture in which slaves did much of the hand labor. That first institution of higher education in the West instilled in academics a deep bias against the making of forms, as opposed to the thinking about Form.[5] Here, too, design thinking flies in the face of that mind–body split. Design involves an iterative process of thinking in the act of making and of making as an act of thinking, and it encompasses both the making of things and the things themselves, the environments of daily life as well as the ideas that underlie them.

That process of thinking and making also involves another skill: problem seeking. Other fields, like literature and philosophy, have a history of envisioning utopias, idealized futures that overcome the perceived problems of the present. Most of those utopias, however, remain thought experiments, and in the rare instance where people have actually tried to put utopian ideas into practice, it has often turned into a nightmarish dystopia because of the lack of critical assessment of the possible problems and their potential downsides. Designers also envision idealized futures, but along with that visioning comes a set of critical skills in how to assess the shortcomings and potential liabilities of every scenario we create. The often perceptive and sometimes picky criticism that occurs in design juries and journals can seem brutal to non-designers, but it is essential in ensuring the appropriateness and responsiveness of the solutions that designers devise.

Design, in sum, involves a particular kind of lateral, expansive, speculative, iterative, and skeptical thinking that can handle high levels of ambiguity and uncertainty. But how, exactly, do designers think when they work? How do they come up with new ideas or imagine environments that don't yet exist? Most designers use analogies, looking for something new based on its similarities with what we already know. The analogies may be more visual than verbal, and more figural than literal in nature, and the connections may arise from within design or from other fields. But designers get good at finding productive analogies and practical parallels.

They do so through the use of techniques common to all creative fields. These include:

- transference—taking something from one context and applying it to another;

- rescaling—transforming something by interpreting it at a very different size;
- inversion—flipping something metaphorically on its head or turning it inside out;
- reassembly—chopping something up and rearranging it for a new purpose or potential.

These and other tools enable designers to envision possibilities and alternative scenarios, seeing beyond what is to what could be. The designer's skill in doing so has become particularly important in the world in which we find ourselves, where we need to create a greener economy, more resilient infrastructure, and a more adaptable physical environment if we are to accommodate the needs of a growing human population threatened by dwindling resources and a decaying natural environment. Never has the imagining and testing of alternative futures been more pressing than it is now.

Every design amounts to what is essentially a "what if" experiment, based on what we know about the needs of particular people and environments and the conditions of a particular place and time. We have generally not seen design in that way. Instead, most of us view design as a subjective activity, a matter of personal taste in what we buy, use, and occupy. As such, design seems outside of the realm of serious discussion, more something that we do in our spare time, when we shop or decorate our houses, rather than a central part of everything we do. This all contributes to the disconnect we suffer with now, between the poor design decisions made by those who don't think of what they do as design, and the disastrous outcomes that have resulted from those decisions.

In science, almost all experiments happen in controlled laboratory settings, so that if an experiment fails—as they often do—no one gets hurt and we can learn from the failure in order to conduct a more successful experiment next time. In design, though, we have few laboratories. Design experiments, in contrast, often happen at full scale and in real time, with the potential for great harm and tremendous cost should they fail—as they sometimes do. Many of the

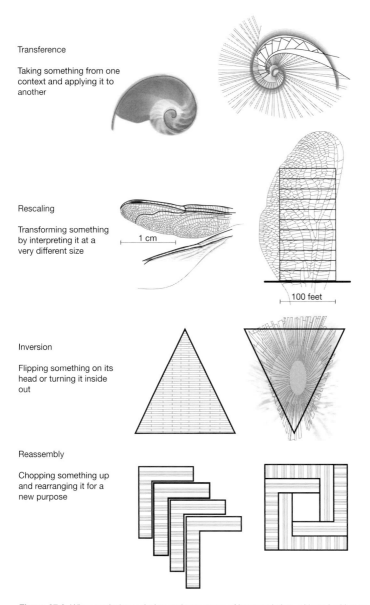

Transference

Taking something from one context and applying it to another

Rescaling

Transforming something by interpreting it at a very different size

1 cm

100 feet

Inversion

Flipping something on its head or turning it inside out

Reassembly

Chopping something up and rearranging it for a new purpose

Figure 27.3 When we judge a design at the moment of its completion, without looking at its potential limitations or shortcomings over time, we flirt with disasters such as the ones we have experienced recently

human-generated disasters we have witnessed in recent years show the catastrophic nature of design experiments gone awry. Never drilled oil wells over a mile underwater? Never allowed minimally regulated sub-prime mortgages? Never pumped so much carbon into the atmosphere before? No problem. We've already conducted those experiments on ourselves and we have learned just how destructive their failure can be.

Because we don't recognize these and other disasters as failed design experiments, we also don't talk about the failures as scientists do theirs. Politicians call hearings, the media seeks blame, the public demands compensation, and those responsible for the failures point fingers at others, but too few of us try to understand the deeper, systemic error from which many of these disasters arise. Instead, we make a few more laws, invest in some new technology, increase regulations as much as politically possible, maybe fire a few scapegoats, and hope that the disaster won't happen again. But all too often, the thinking behind the catastrophe remains unchanged, and we go on conducting deadly experiments on ourselves and on the natural environment.

Were we to operate as the scientific community does when conducting and evaluating experiments, we would require ample documentation, without claims of proprietary information; demand their replication, without allowing things to go live ahead of time; and disseminate the findings through peer-reviewed journals, before we go to market. These procedures, of course, occur in some parts of the marketplace where not doing so can have immediately deadly results: in the design of vehicles, for example, or pharmaceuticals. But we often overlook the equally deadly results of untested experiments in most other parts of the marketplace. Did we think, when we developed automobiles, that not only would the vehicles themselves become the single greatest cause of deaths among young people between ages 15 and 24, but also that they would fragment communities, isolate families, contaminate the air, and contribute to the pollution of our waterways and the fragmentation of other species' habitat?[6] And the automobile remains just one of many grand experiments we have enacted upon ourselves, the results of which have begun to come in. The question is: do we continue to do this to our planet and to ourselves, or can we change our perspective and design our world in a different way?

28

The Logic of Design

Designers, as a group, tend to have strong visual and spatial skills, and the ability to think simultaneously in two and three dimensions, at various scales and from different perspectives at the same time, with drawing and diagramming as essential tools to convey their ideas. But while that visual and spatial intelligence occurs in some people more strongly than in others, it also constitutes one of the eight forms of intelligence that psychologist Howard Gardner has identified in his theory of multiple intelligences (linguistic, logical/mathematical, musical, visual/spatial, body/kinesthetic, interpersonal, intrapersonal, naturalist) and so it exists in almost everyone to some degree.[1] Navigating the three-dimensional world would be nearly impossible without it. That, in turn, suggests that virtually everyone can learn at least the basic components of design thinking and how to apply it to their work, however non-visual or non-spatial they might be.

In the spirit of visualizing the invisible, what does design thinking look like? How would we diagram it and what can we learn about it by thinking about it not as some ephemeral or mysterious process, but as a three-dimensional object? Such questions suggest that diagramming design thinking itself remains a design problem. As in every other design act, conceiving what design thinking looks like demands an iterative process that will undoubtedly improve the diagram as the result of critique and subsequent redesign. But all design starts somewhere, and so the following figure represents an initial idea for consideration.

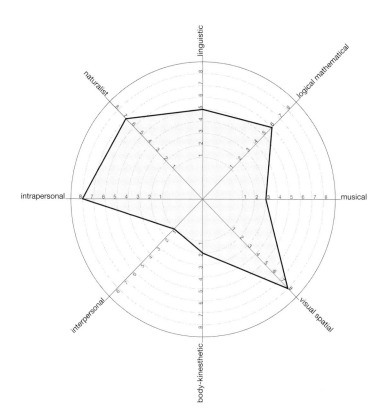

Figure 28.1 Visual and spatial intelligence occurs in some people more strongly than in others, it also constitutes one of the eight that psychologist Howard Gardner has identified in his theory of multiple intelligences and so exists in almost everyone to some degree.

Look at this in relation to inductive and deductive thinking.[2] We can think of those two forms of logic moving in opposite directions along a triangle. Deduction works from an initial premise and draws from it either valid or invalid conclusions based on the truth of that premise or on the logic of the reasoning involved in coming to those conclusions. We might diagram it as a process that starts at the top of the triangle, from a set of premises assumed to be true, with many possible conclusions flowing in diverse directions from that point. Mathematics typically entails such deductive reasoning. From a set of axioms or definitions, mathematicians can generate conclusions that logically follow from the premises.

Induction moves in the other direction. It starts from empirical observations of phenomena or experiences and, based on that activity, constructs one or more general theories or laws that have a high probability of explaining the properties or relationships of the things observed. As we know from science, the test of induction comes from the ability to repeat an experiment, observe the same phenomena, and arrive at the same conclusions predicted by the theory. From the multiple occurrences or experiences in our lives

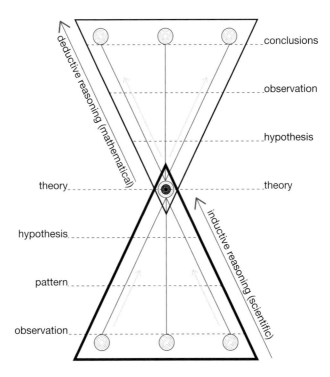

Figure 28.2 The inductive/deductive triangle. Deduction works from an initial premise and draws from it either valid or invalid conclusions based on the truth of that premise. Induction starts from empirical observations of phenomena or experiences and based on that activity, constructs general theories that have a high probability of explanation.

and that form the base of our triangle, induction focuses on some in order to draw a conclusion that, like the point of the triangle, has a high degree of stability and explanatory power.

Abduction takes a very different form.[3] First, it doesn't move vertically up or down the pyramid of reasoning like induction or deduction. Instead abduction moves laterally, typically making analogies between seemingly unrelated phenomena or disconnected things in order to draw new and often unexpected conclusions that might be useful in a particular situation. Such lateral or analogical thinking involves a form of induction, in that it draws conclusions from observed phenomena. But unlike induction, it doesn't seek general laws or universal principles, instead it connects particular things in order to solve specific problems in a given time and place. This is what design thinking does and why it remains different from mathematics and science, and yet as essential to our ability to live in and understand the world.

Second, abductive reasoning does not have the linear direction that we often associate with induction and deduction. Instead, design thinking has a spiraling or looping form, in which, faced with a problem to solve or a need to serve, we make an initial step based on our understanding of the situation, and then test that first scheme in terms of how well it addresses the problem or need. Even the most skilled designers find that that preliminary hunch needs revision of some sort and so the process involves both looping back to re-examine the problem and gathering more information about it and its context in order to move forward toward a better solution.

That looping back and expanding out can seem disturbing to those who think that, inductively or deductively, solutions should follow logically and linearly from a problem. The abductive process may look undisciplined or uncertain as it takes a step back or broadens out its perspective, but that spiraling motion, in fact, provides a way of ensuring that the ultimate solution satisfies as many of the needs and accounts for as many of the considerations as simply and efficiently as possible. Abductive thinkers know that to go forward they also have to go backward, and that to arrive at the best answer, they also need to consider more possibilities than a linear approach to a problem might suggest.

Indeed, the lateral, loopy, and undulating form that results from this process highlights the reason why we have suffered from so much poor design and such catastrophic failures in areas where people have not followed this path. Dealing with design problems in a reductive or linear way, as if every problem has a simple and logical solution, eliminates what remains most valuable about the design process: the continual self-criticism and collective critique that forces the designer to go back and reconsider. That critical examination occurs at every point in the diagram where the process loops back and/or expands out, and the more that happens—within reason—the better the results and, more importantly, the less likely they will lead to a catastrophic failure. No process, of course, is perfect; design flaws do occur and product failures do happen. Such setbacks, however, typically stem from a design process cut too short or followed too fast, reducing the number of critiques, the range of input, or the time to completion to the point where flaws got through or possible failures did not get caught.

When allowed the time it needs, however, and when given the support it takes to do it right, the abductive design process has evolved over the course of human history to ensure the best results given the problem at hand and the resources available. Bad design occurs not only when the results fail, or at least fail to live up to our expectation or to meet our needs. Bad design also happens when something costs too much or wastes too much or takes too much to make. While the design process does not lead to a true or verifiable conclusion, as happens with deduction or induction, it does generate a limited number of optimal solutions that address the greatest number of issues in the most elegant and efficient way.

29

The Pragmatics of Design

The value of abduction lies in its consequences, as Charles Sanders Peirce, the nineteenth-century American philosopher, argued.[1] The lateral connections that abductive thinking—design thinking—makes can be very productive or completely meaningless depending upon its results. The key question is: did a creative insight lead to something useful or not? Peirce called this judging of things according to their consequences "pragmatism." Critics of pragmatism have argued that we can never know the full consequences of things in the future, and so we have no way to measure their pragmatic value. Designers have likewise shown a degree of skepticism about judging their work based on long-term consequences, given the relative lack of time and attention given to the assessment of design objects, systems, and environments after the fact by designers themselves. That may stem from the long-held prejudice in the larger culture that design and creativity in general remain intuitive and inexplicable. But even the most cursory investigation of abduction shows that that is not the case. Abduction involves a highly disciplined way of discovering new knowledge and developing new ideas.

Educational psychologists Gary Shank and Donald J. Cunningham have developed a more nuanced way of thinking about abduction, showing how abductive thinking and research proceeds in an orderly and methodical way toward the development of useful inferences.[2] The six modes of inferences that Shank and Cunningham identified describe, in different words, the design process. But Shank and Cunningham's analysis of abduction also shows how the design process constitutes a type of discovery that can produce results as valuable as anything coming out of a scientific lab or off a mathematician's blackboard. While we can't know what Peirce, who died in 1914, would have thought about this, it does seem very much in line with his pragmatic temper, which embraced all thinking that helps us solve problems and get on with life. Indeed, Shank and Cunningham's work is, itself, abductive—a creative leap that connects seemingly unrelated ideas to create something new and useful.

The six classes of inferences or ways in which we draw conclusions about the world, according to Shank and Cunningham, are:

1 Omen or Hunch, when we have an intuition about some possibility.
2 Symptom, when we find in that intuition a resemblance to other things.
3 Metaphor or Analogy, when we see clear parallels to things we already know.
4 Clue, when we relate the specifics of the particular case to more general solutions.
5 Diagnosis or Scenario, when we apply it as a prototype to more than the particular case.
6 Explanation, when we evolve a theory from the particular case that can apply to all cases.[3]

When working on a project or problem, an experienced designer will often have a hunch that an idea will work to organize and make sense of the diversity of requirements. That hunch usually arises out of aspects of the problem that are symptomatic of other, similar problems the designer has faced, from which parallels get drawn. The design will then typically evolve in an analogous or metaphorical way, in which ideas about what we already know or have already solved get applied to the new situation, changing in the process and becoming a new gestalt. As the design proceeds, other clues emerge that suggest

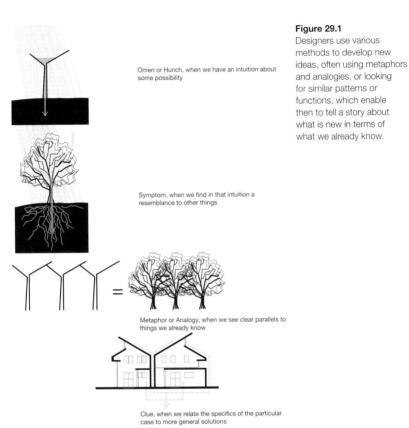

Omen or Hunch, when we have an intuition about some possibility

Symptom, when we find in that intuition a resemblance to other things

Metaphor or Analogy, when we see clear parallels to things we already know

Clue, when we relate the specifics of the particular case to more general solutions

Diagnosis or Scenario, when we apply it as a prototype to more than the particular case

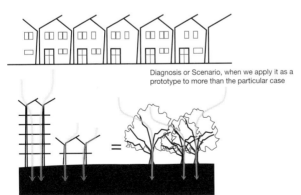

Explanation, when we evolve a theory from the particular case that can apply to all cases

Figure 29.1
Designers use various methods to develop new ideas, often using metaphors and analogies, or looking for similar patterns or functions, which enable then to tell a story about what is new in terms of what we already know.

new applications of the idea, beyond what has happened before, which eventually leads to more general scenarios and possibly to a broader theory that can be of use to others when confronting the same sort of problem.

Shank and Cunningham do more, here, than simply put into new words what designers already do. They help us see that there exist at least six distinct ways in which creative ideas can emerge, and as a result, at least six different ways in which designers proceed to work. As a set of disciplines, the design community has long been accustomed to judging something based on its success in meeting a need, but rarely do we look at the consequences of what we do in terms of the inferences we make. What difference does it make, in other words, to work from a hunch, as opposed to seeking an omen, looking for symptoms, applying a metaphor, drawing an analogy, responding to clues, making a diagnosis, envisioning a scenario, or offering an explanation? Do certain starting points lend themselves better to some situations rather than others? Do some produce better results than others? Are they all equally valid or simply a matter of personal preference, or does each mode of inference have strengths and weaknesses?

Such questions are not simply of academic interest. Research into the nature of designers' abductive thinking can go a long way toward helping others not only understand the value of design, but also understand the importance that different approaches to design thinking has in terms of end results as well as in terms of the role design thinking plays in the conduct of research. Abduction, as Peirce observed, serves as the prelude to all other research; without it, induction and deduction would not occur, for the latter would not have the hunches that lead to the hypotheses from which to proceed.[4]

This, in turn, suggests that the design community has too narrowly defined what it does in terms of the products of its actions. We have legally determined that only people licensed to design buildings can call themselves architects, for example. But were we to understand the nature of the inferences designers make, we would see that this mode of thinking has applications far beyond the products and environments that we have associated with design for so long. Abductive reasoning gives designers the capacity not only to solve problems in the physical world related to people's material needs, but also to see what Peirce called "firstness": the potentiality of and in things.[5] Every new design creates something that didn't exist before and juxtaposes entities never brought together before in the same space and time. As such, it creates potential opportunities for us to relate to others in new ways, improving the effect that we have on other people, other species, future generations, and the planet as a whole.

This runs counter to the prejudice of some people who see designers as impractical or unable to stay on schedule or in budget — all characteristics of a bad designer. Design, when done well, meets a need well, with a practical, durable, and affordable result. And when done poorly, we get the kind of disastrous failures we have seen in our financial industry, our housing industry, our oil industry — to name just a few. Many have tried to pin these failures on corrupt officials, cowardly consultants, contemptuous corporate bosses, or incompetent workers. But no amount of careful fabrication and maintenance can compensate for not understanding the nature of abductive reasoning and not seeing the bad design that can result from that misunderstanding. So while most people are not and never will be professional designers, everyone faced with creating something new, something to meet a new need or address a new problem, will think like a designer. And when we do that well, we can begin to create a more durable, resilient, cost-effective, and failure-resistant world, quite unlike the world that we have constructed, over the last century, at our peril.

30

The Holon of Design

We might also begin to understand the larger relevance of design thinking—not only as a tool to create useful things, but also as a way of being in the world. To see that, let's imagine turning the undulating, spiraling design process ninety degrees and looking at it on-end. We would see a series of connected loops nested within each other, with some of the spirals more tightly wound and others less so, as the design process narrowed in and then expanded out along its course. The backward loops that seem such a disorienting aspect of the design process, as we take a step back in order to move forward, have largely disappeared in this end view. Instead, the connection among the various levels or scales at which the design process occurs has become more prominent. What seemed loose and even somewhat disorganized from the side, now appears to move in a much tighter and more integrated way from an end view.

That end view reveals the design process as what Arthur Koestler called a "holon." Koestler argued that everything exists simultaneously as an independent whole made up of parts and as parts of a larger whole.[1] This seems like a fairly obvious idea when we stop to think about it. Nature contains holons across every scale, from atoms that exist as wholes and also as parts of molecular wholes that exist as parts of cellular wholes that exist as parts of organisms and so on. The same holds true for the built world. A doorknob, while a whole, also exists as part of a door that, while a whole, also exists as part of

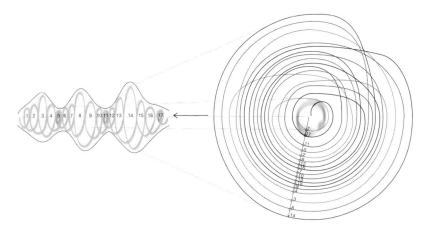

Figure 30.1 The holon of design. The connection among the various levels or scales at which the design process occurs makes it a "holon," a word coined by Arthur Koestler to describe the reality in which we live, where everything is at once a whole made up of parts and a part of a larger whole.

a wall that, while a whole, also exists as part of a room, as part of a building, as part of a neighborhood, and so on.

Many of the conflicts in the world arise, as Koestler noted, from our not recognizing everything's simultaneous "both–and" existence.[2] Prejudice and hate, ignorance and fear, exploitation and repression, war and violence—almost every ill we can imagine stems from people not seeing their inseparability, interdependence, and absolute reliance on each other and on all of the other species on the planet, however foreign they may appear. At the same time, a "holonistic" view of the world recognizes the distinction between parts—between individuals in a society, details in a composition, components of a system—and doesn't lose sight of them by over-emphasizing the whole. Abduction, as a form of reasoning that sees relationships among seemingly unrelated things, and design, as a process that constructs such relationships, both reinforce this holonistic worldview.

An end view of the design process shows how. As the design process spirals outward and inward, forward and backward toward the optimal solutions to problems, it also links everything that it encounters and reveals those connections in a well-resolved final product. Bad design, on the other hand, like poor reasoning, makes artificial divisions, false distinctions, and forced separations among things and therein lays the source of many catastrophic collapses and devastating disasters we have experienced of late. These failures have occurred not just because of shoddy construction, poor maintenance, and unregulated greed, but also come from a fundamental misunderstanding of the profoundly interconnected "holonistic" nature of the world.

A holonistic view of things also shows, in specific ways, how failures occur. One common error, evident in totalitarian systems of all sorts, involves too strong a focus on the whole, without enough attention paid to the wholeness of the parts that comprise it. This leads, in politics, to the repression of individuals on behalf of some group, nation, or ideal, seeing people as means to some larger end. We also see this in the design of things, environments, and systems. The dismissal or lack of attention to parts or details often serves as a prelude to disaster. Think of the inspectors who overlooked the overstressed gusset plate that brought down the I-35W Bridge, the engineers whose over-dependence on the blow-out protector led to the BP oil spill, or the over-confidence of the designers of the aging levee system prior to the flooding of New Orleans after Katrina. Whether involving people or things, political systems or infrastructural ones, too great a focus on the whole to the detriment of the parts will inevitably bring the whole down. Wholes depend on their parts and only by recognizing the wholeness of each part and by valuing each part (or person as Kant said) as an end itself, and not as a means to other ends, will the larger whole survive.[3]

Attending to the parts to the detriment of the whole also presents a problem. Like libertarian politics, with its pitting of individual freedom against the good of the group, paying too much attention to the parts without seeing their dependence on the larger whole can also lead to disaster. Unlike the break in an overlooked part that brings down the whole in a fracture-critical collapse, the fracturing or fragmentation of the whole can make it impossible for the parts to thrive. The heroic individualism that has fueled much of the anti-

government rhetoric of recent years remains stubbornly, and sometimes stupidly, blind to all the ways in which individuals depend on
the government—and on larger wholes of all sorts, including communities and the natural environment. Neglecting those wholes by
too fiercely focusing on the parts underlies the collapse of the
financial industry and the bursting of the housing bubble, in which
individual greed trumped the collective good, harming a great
number of people as a result.

While apparently opposed to each other, the extreme collectivist
and the extreme individualist make the same mistake from a

Over-emphasis on the
whole leads to neglect of
the parts.

Over-emphasis on the
parts leads to neglect
of the whole.

Figure 30.2 Totalitarian systems focus too strongly on the whole, without enough attention
paid to the parts that comprise it, while libertarian systems pay too much attention to the
parts without seeing their dependence on the larger whole. Both lead to disaster.

holonistic perspective. Both pay too much attention to one level of the holon and disconnect it from other levels, either smaller-scale parts or larger-scale wholes. And because of that disconnection, stresses in systems that would normally get absorbed across the holon, from one level to another, can lead to sudden and unexpected collapses: fracture-critical failures. That such failures almost never occur in nature stems from the holon-like connections within and among ecosystems, distributing stresses and mitigating impacts so that the whole remains healthy even as some parts wane and others thrive. The flaw in fracture-critical systems has as much to do with our thinking as with our actions. Whenever we see a system, at any level, as separate from others either larger or smaller in scale, we set ourselves up for the catastrophes we have begun to experience with ever-greater frequency. And the way to avoid disasters in the future lies in reconnecting the parts and wholes of the holon that comprises the world.

That seems so simple. Why, then, don't we make these connections and be done with it? The answer lies in the fact that maintaining a disconnect among the different scales and in the different realms in which we live provides an advantage to some over others. As humans, for example, we have long focused on our species and viewed other species as available for our use and exploitation, a disconnection with the world around us that has begun to threaten us as the ecosystems upon which we depend for our food and water have begun to collapse. By not seeing ourselves as part of the larger whole of the planet, our wholeness as a species has become endangered.

The same occurs at smaller scales as well. Individuals, who seek to take advantage of others, legally or illegally, have disconnected themselves, at least in their own minds, from the larger consequences of that behavior. People can try to justify the exploitation of others in the name of free-market competition or the survival of the fittest, but in the end the holonistic nature of reality means that, eventually, the negative effects of their actions turn on them. Of course, the word "eventually" matters a lot in many people's minds.

If they can achieve a short-term gain at the expense of others, they will take their chances over the long term that they can avoid future losses or put them off long enough that it won't matter.

That may have worked in the nineteenth and early twentieth centuries, when travel and communication still took a long time. People could distance themselves from the negative consequences of bad behavior and ignore the "moral sentiment"—to use Adam Smith's term—that kept such behavior in check when people lived within sight of those who they might want to exploit.[4] But global communications have made it ever harder to escape the effects of predatory actions. Look at how quickly an incendiary act in one part of the world can go viral and prompt angry protests in another, as happened when the minister of a tiny church in Florida, proposing to burn a stack of Korans, ignited global protests.[5] At the same time, the scale at which we now work in the modern world magnifies the consequences of bad behavior. What might have had limited impact in previous eras can now, because of our technological prowess, have large-scale and long-term devastating effects on millions of people. Consider the impact that the collapse of a couple of New York investment banks had on the global financial system.

In the end, the fracture-critical catastrophes we have endured raise ethical questions as much as they do design issues. The fundamental charge in ethics of seeing the world from the perspective of another and treating others as we would want them to treat us leads almost inevitably toward a holonistic way of thinking about design. By seeing the world as a continuously linked reality, in which every action affects every part that comprises the whole as well as the larger whole of which it is a part, we recognize how much everything we do affects us as well as others, and that, in the end, we can never escape the negative consequences of our actions for ourselves.

31

Designing Our Future

What does this mean for architects and designers? While the architectural and design community remains broadly interested and generally engaged in sustainable design, the issue of equity poses an awkward dilemma. Because most architects and designers depend upon the wealthy and powerful for work, we have little incentive to embrace the idea that we may never achieve a more sustainable future unless we also create a more equitable one. When ecologist William Rees gave a talk at the national convention of the American Institute of Architects (AIA), he told the crowd of several thousand architects they need to reduce the environmental impact of buildings by 90 percent over the next fifty years.[1] He received enthusiastic applause from the audience of architects, but from what I could see and hear from the conversations afterward, it seemed as if the enormity of what Rees said did not register with most in the audience.

Achieving such reductions will take much more than increasing the use of "green" materials or of energy-conserving mechanical systems or appliances. A 90 percent reduction demands a wholesale change in how we live and how much we consume, an issue that few architects probably want to raise with our clients. Many in the profession might agree with Tony Judt of the Remarque Institute: "The American pursuit of wealth, size, and abundance—as material surrogates for happiness—is aesthetically unpleasing and ecologically catastrophic."[2] But architects are often complicit in creating those material surrogates—buildings of great cost, size, and abundance—with our fees often going up accordingly. To create a more sustainable, equitable world, we may need to begin by taking a hard look at how we practice and at how we, as a profession, contribute to the problem.

Richard Farson mused as he stepped down as the public member of the AIA board in 2003:

> I sometimes wonder what an American architect would say if approached by the leader of China seeking his or her help for the 800 million ill-housed, struggling Chinese. "Well, the way we believe residential architecture should be practiced is that each home should be custom designed, the architect should be an integral part of the process for each structure, from beginning to end, carefully surveying the site, designing a structure that is particularly suited for that site, working intensively with the client to understand that individual's special needs, making sure that the contractors are performing, and that the project is completed on budget. Normally it takes us about a year or so to finish such a project, and we can undertake perhaps ten a year. We don't condone selling stock plans. But we could bring a thousand architects to work with you." The leader would shake his head, concluding that such a program, even if China could afford it, would take 800 years.[3]

Farson ended his talk by calling for architects to become "meta-designers," focused less on the design of individual buildings and more on orchestrating a wide range of other disciplines to help address the problems of the built environment. Even more controversially, he argued: "architecture should be publicly supported in the same way that education and medicine are. Our professional strategies should include making a case for major public funding, to the tune of trillions of dollars over time."[4]

Large-scale public funding of the profession is not likely to happen soon, but Farson's observations show how our dominant mode of practice may no longer align with what the world needs from us. The architect–client relationship works well in situations that call for custom design in response to individual needs, but in cases like the Chinese example Farson gives — or now, given China's rise, Africa or other parts of Asia — that form of practice seems wildly impractical. What we need, instead, is a variant of architecture and design that produces building- and infrastructure-scale prototypes within meta-designed systems and organizations that can adapt to particular places and to the capacities of particular groups of people. The design professions, however, have yet to design the mechanisms that could make this happen at a large scale. It requires some combination of industrial design, architecture, engineering, anthropology, and global studies, able to develop widely applicable, culturally appropriate, and locally produced prototypes and projects.

This "public-interest design," as some have called it,[5] is not only relevant to the most impoverished nations. With ever-more intense weather brought on by global climate change affecting most parts of the world, people all over the planet will soon find themselves in need of such humanitarian efforts. As MIT scientist Kerry Emanuel has shown, tropical storms now last half as long again and generate winds 50 percent more powerful than just a few decades ago, the result of ever-warmer tropical seas.[6] And with rapidly increasing populations living in vulnerable areas, we could see a whole new category of the homeless, "environmental refugees," as Oxford scientist Norman Myers calls them, with "as many as 200 million people overtaken by disruptions of monsoon systems and other rainfall regimes, by droughts of unprecedented severity and duration, and by sea-level rise and coastal flooding."[7]

How should we respond to such a sobering prospect, affecting developed, developing, and undeveloped countries alike? It may be, at least in the short term, that architects can work best as independent, creative entrepreneurs in partnership with the public and non-profit entities dedicated to helping the growing number of people rendered homeless or placeless because of environmental or economic dislocation. Some architects have begun to do just that. They have addressed different aspects of the sustainability-and-equity problem—the infrastructure needs of slum dwellers, the shelter needs of the homeless, the material needs of those with few resources, and the habitation needs of those on the move. What unites their work is not just a commitment to environmental sustainability and social equity, but also an underlying and often unstated vision of the future that brings us back to where we have spent most of our history as a species: living in a highly mobile and nimble way, building with what is at hand, improving the environment around us, and occupying the land so lightly that we hardly leave a trace.

The United Nations' Millennium Development Goals call for significant improvement of the lives of at least 100 million of the world's two billion slum dwellers by 2020, focusing on access to safe drinking water and sanitation.[8] With those goals in mind, architect John Gavin Dwyer and his former firm, Shelter, have designed a self-contained structure able to provide global slum-dwellers what they often need the most: access to electricity, clean water, and toilet and bathing facilities.[9] Called the "Clean Hub," the 10 foot by 20 foot unit has a metal roof that collects rainwater, an adjustable array of photovoltaic panels able to generate up to 2,640 watts of electricity, a reverse-osmosis water system that cleans water stored in a below-ground reservoir, showers and sinks whose grey water gets recycled back to the reservoir, and waterless, self-composting toilets. The building itself has impact-resistant stress-skin walls and has secure entry doors, supported by a steel-tube and concrete-pier foundation that can adjust to sloped terrain and poor soil. The Clean Hub's expected thirty-year life makes it most suitable for the many semi-permanent slums around the world that lack basic infrastructure.

Addressing the needs of people who have lost their housing during hurricanes and earthquakes involves another kind of response. Cameron Sinclair and Kate Stohr's organization Architecture for Humanity has shown how much architects have to contribute in the wake of these disasters.[10] When Hurricane Ivan destroyed 85 percent of Grenada in 2004, and Hurricane Emily did further damage in

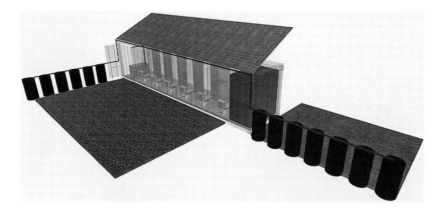

Figure 31.1 The "Clean Hub" is a 10 foot by 20 foot unit with a metal roof that collects rainwater, an adjustable array of photovoltaic panels to generate electricity, a reverse-osmosis water system to clean water, showers and sinks whose grey water gets recycled, and waterless, self-composting toilets.

2005, for example, Architecture for Humanity participated in a team that included Arquitectonica, Ferrara Design, and Grenada Relief, Recovery and Reconstruction (GR3), producing seventy prototype transitional housing units. Called Global Village Shelters and designed by Daniel and Mia Ferrara of Ferrera Design, the temporary houses are made from recycled corrugated cardboard impregnated to be fire retardant and laminated for water resistance.

Architecture for Humanity has also addressed the needs of people suffering from war or disease. In the organization's 1999 competition for housing for returning wartime refuges in Kosovo, architects such as Sean Godsell developed his "future shack," using a standard shipping container and an unfolding roof to provide shade. In 2003, Architecture for Humanity sponsored a design competition for a mobile HIV/AIDS clinic for Africa, with KHRAS Architects designing the first place entry, with a metal-framed, self-contained, lockable structure that also incorporates local materials. And, with students from the University of Minnesota's School of Architecture, they designed and arranged to build a prototypical laundry building in Mississippi, to serve people living without

Figure 31.2 With students from the University of Minnesota, Architecture for Humanity designed and arranged to build a prototypical laundry building in Lakeland, Mississippi, to serve people after Katrina and to provide a gathering place in communities that had lost their public infrastructure.

washers and dryers in emergency trailers after Katrina and to provide a gathering place in communities that had lost their public infrastructure.

Other organizations, such as Design Corps, founded by Bryan Bell, and Public Architecture, established by John Peterson, have focused more of their efforts on the chronically impoverished in the United States. Design Corps has developed prototypical farmworker housing that is as easily moved as the migrant laborers it seeks to accommodate. By engaging in community design, offering design build courses for students, and organizing an annual conference for those working in this area, Design Corps has also become a major force in the public-interest architecture movement.[11]

John Peterson's Public Architecture has taken a somewhat different tack. It has tried to leverage the talents of the U.S. architectural community to do pro bono work through the 1 percent program, which asks architects to give one percent of their time to public-interest design. The success of that effort has been extraordinary, and it shows how much people want to contribute if given the chance. Public Architecture has also conducted some notable competitions for facilities that almost never get the attention of the design community, such as the day laborer stations that will provide shelter, off-the-grid power, and employment and meeting space for this important workforce.[12]

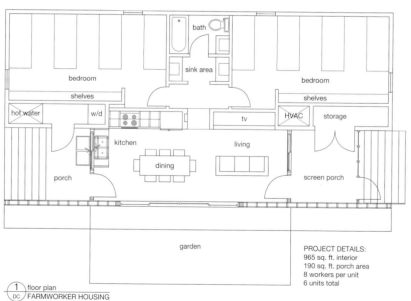

bath

sink area

bedroom

shelves

bedroom

shelves

hot water

w/d

kitchen

tv

HVAC

storage

living

dining

porch

screen porch

garden

PROJECT DETAILS:
965 sq. ft. interior
190 sq. ft. porch area
8 workers per unit
6 units total

1 floor plan
DC FARMWORKER HOUSING

Figure 31.3 Design Corps has developed prototypical farmworker housing as mobile as the migrant laborers it accommodates. By engaging in community design and by offering design build courses and an annual conference, Design Corps has also become a major force in the public-interest design movement.

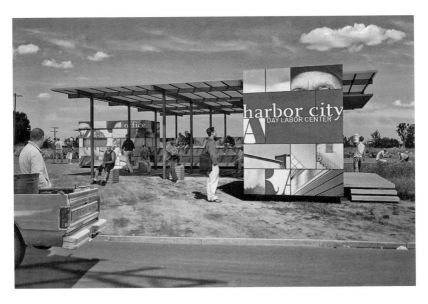

Figure 31.4 Public Architecture has focused on the design of facilities that almost never get the attention of the design community, such as the day laborer stations that will provide shelter, off-the-grid power, and employment and meeting space for this important workforce.

Other architects have begun to look at unconventional materials as low-cost, sustainable alternatives to what the market has to offer. Richard Kroeker and students at Dalhousie and Minnesota have worked with aboriginal and native communities to adopt indigenous approaches to construction using pliable wood materials in various woven and tied configurations drawn from what is immediately available on or near a site. He has also begun to look at materials in the modern waste stream, such as unused telephone books held in compression to form bearing walls of a "phone book building."[13]

Another architect working in this area is Wes Janz, whose students at Ball State, along with I-Beam Design, have developed ways to use the 1.9 million wood pallets destined for landfills in the United States for housing, drawing on the widespread use of pallets in squatter housing around the world. These examples and others in his exhibition and book, *OneSmallProject*, revise the ancient idea that

Figure 31.5 Richard Kroeker and his students at Dalhousie University have begun to look at materials in the modern waste stream, such as unused telephone books held in compression to form bearing walls of a "phone book building," whose massive walls also provide ample insulation.

we build with what we have at hand, and that we empower people to build for themselves.[14]

All of these efforts suggest a new kind of practice for architects, based on advocacy, activism, and attention to what the rest of the world wastes. However, these architectural inventions have, so far, remained largely research. If we are going to create a more sustainable and equitable world, we need to apply these lessons on a broader scale, to people of all types. How might these examples serve not only the world's billions of slum dwellers, and potentially its millions of environmental refugees, but also the developed world, where some of the greatest inequity and unsustainability occur? For that, we need to rethink the social contract we have related to equity and the environment.

Figure 31.6 House with Sleeping Loft, Pallet Structure #3. Wes Janz's students at Ball State University, along with I-Beam Design, have developed ways to use the 1.9 million wood pallets destined for landfills in the United States for housing, drawing on the widespread use of pallets in squatter housing around the world.

32

What We Can Live Without

Historically, we have thought of that social contract in two very different ways. The seventeenth-century philosopher Thomas Hobbes imagined a life in the "state of nature" as one that he famously characterized as "nasty, brutish, and short," a condition of constant warfare "of every man, against every man."[1] He argued that, because of these inequalities in nature, humans entered into a social contract to create powerful central authorities—the Leviathan, as he called it—in order to achieve the equality and security that he thought impossible living close to nature.

The eighteenth-century philosopher Jean-Jacques Rousseau imagined just the opposite. He envisioned the "state of nature" as one characterized by the peaceful co-existence of equals, who lived with abundance and with little need for property. Conflict arose, according to Rousseau, the first time someone put a stake in the ground and claimed land as their own, leading to the inequities of property ownership and the need for a social contract that would protect people's rights, while maximizing our personal freedom.[2]

Political theorists still study Hobbes and Rousseau, finding in their work justification for authoritarian or libertarian ideologies, respectively. But we can learn something else from them: what it means to imagine a "state of nature" in today's world, given the unsustainable and inequitable ways in which we now live in North America. Both Hobbes and Rousseau saw nature in much the same way: as a near infinite resource that is there for our use. And both saw equity in terms of property and political power, a matter of law and regulation. We now know, however, that the natural environment is anything but infinite, and that our fate, as a species, is intimately connected with its health. At the same time, we now know that equity takes many different forms, only some of which have to do with property and political power.

A new social contract, based on how we know the world to be, would have almost the opposite characteristics of those we have inherited from Hobbes and Rousseau. It would be a contract that recognizes and rewards people according to how well they husband finite resources, improve the natural environment, serve those most in need, and give as much as possible to others. Equity would no longer be, as it was for Hobbes and Rousseau, primarily a matter of keeping greed in check, since that assumes that the primary motive of human action is to acquire as much property or power as possible. In the new social contract, freedom would not consist of how much property we can own, instead it would be a matter of how much we can live without, as Thoreau said,[3] and equity would be a matter of how much we can "live simply so that others may simply live," as Gandhi is credited with having said. In a future in which many of us may be on the move, living lightly has real advantages.

This, of course, sounds impractical, idealistic, and naive in our ego-driven, winner-takes-all world, but it is anything but that. It is the most practical, pragmatic, and realistic alternative we have at a time when we have just a few generations to avoid the kind of environmental collapse and subsequent social turmoil that an increasing number see in our future. If we are to meet William Rees's challenge of reducing our impact on the environment by 90 percent in fifty years, and if we are to make marked improvements on the dozen factors Jared Diamond sees as our greatest threats, we need to transform what we value, how we share, and who we embrace in the global community.

Our history and recent practices suggest that we will default to either Hobbes's or Rousseau's idea of the social contract, with some advocating for a strong authority imposing controls through strict regulation and others calling for a libertarian loosening of restrictions in order to maximize individual freedom. But at a time of rapidly growing population—estimated to be roughly nine billion people before the end of the twenty-first century—and rapidly diminishing resources, neither of these older social contracts work.[4] There will be too large and diverse a population for a singular authority and too few, finite resources for an expansion of personal liberty. The new social contract will require us to internalize that authority and that freedom: to learn, as an essential part of being human, how to value the group as much as the individual, future generations as much as the present, and other species as much as ourselves.

This new contract isn't really new. The three dominant ethical traditions in the West all align with this shift in thinking, as does the work of a growing number of architects. Virtue ethics, with its focus on character traits such as a prudence and justice, demands that we look to the wellbeing of others, and that we live modestly and with humility. The work of the late Samuel Mockbee exemplifies this architecturally. His Rural Studio for Auburn University students has created a number of houses and public buildings for some of the most needy people in one of the poorest counties in the United States. Using recycled materials—such as used tires for walls, reused windshields for windows, and discarded license plates for cladding— the Rural Studio has designed and built some of the most powerful projects of the late twentieth century, showing how what Mockbee called the "old-fashioned virtue" of giving to others can be the basis for the creation of community.[5]

Deontological ethics, with its concern for doing what is right regardless of consequences, reinforces our responsibility toward other species and future generations, and our obligation to act with them always in mind. Such an ethic underlies most utopian thinking, and that tradition remains as a way of showing what a new social contract might look like. Michael Sorkin has taken such an approach, exploring, in a number of urban designs, new forms of

Figure 32.1 The Rural Studio at Auburn University has created a number of houses and public buildings for some of the most needy people in one of the poorest counties in the United States. Their design of a $20,000 house shows how good design can produce more value for less money than a mobile home.

sustainable communities.[6] For example, his Penangs Peaks project—a mixed-use community of housing, offices, and various public and commercial facilities—will be self-sufficient in terms of water and waste management. The project envisions a series of foliage-clad towers arranged around a large park, showing how large numbers of people can live in urban settings with a minimal impact on the local environment.

Finally, utilitarianism, with its goal of maximizing the happiness of as many as possible, demands that we include all other beings in its calculus of the greatest good for the greatest number, with attention to the process and consequences of all that we do. A socially active architect such as Thomas Dutton demonstrates that in his work in Cincinnati's Over-the-Rhine district, with the Over-the-Rhine Housing Network, representing a more participatory approach.[7] He and his Miami University students have designed and renovated a number of living and commercial spaces, including a laundromat, two single-family townhouses, and a number of apartments, with budgets in the $5,000 to $10,000 range. Dutton's students have also explored a kind of guerilla urbanism, using utility trucks to bring information related to poverty to well-to-do parts of town, and using public parks for temporary exhibitions on social justice issues.

Nor is the underpinning for this new social contract strictly secular and ethical. All of the major religious and spiritual traditions in both the East and the West recognize the values we now need to embrace if we are to avoid a global collapse, values such as moderation and self-restraint, charity and mercy. At the heart of almost every religious text lies the message that happiness that comes from giving away what we don't absolutely need, serving as often as possible the poorest and most disadvantaged, and helping others as much as possible, without expectations of anything in return. Myriad religious communities remain the mainstays of housing the homeless, and in so doing show us what we will have to deal with as hundreds of millions of environmental refugees face similar conditions.

The social contract underlying such work will serve us particularly well in what lies ahead. As we saw in the aftermath of the flooding of New Orleans, it was charitable individuals who initially came to the aid of others without regard for who they were. Rugged individualism and enlightened self-interest may work as a social ethic in periods of abundance, but in the coming era of scarce resources, those who value cooperation, interdependence, and mutual aid and who see wealth in non-material, ethical, and spiritual terms, will be the ones who thrive. Such were the values and the wealth of the indigenous people of North America, and if we want to live sustainably on this continent for generations to come, they will need to become ours as well.

And such values also lie deep in Western culture, as the historian David Shi has argued: "the most important historical influence on American simplicity has been the combined heritage of Greco-Roman culture and Judeo-Christian ethics. Most Greek and Roman philosophers were emphatic in their praise of simple living, as were the Hebrew prophets and Jesus."[8] Shi warns that "proponents of the simple life have frequently been overly nostalgic about the quality of life in olden times, narrowly anti-urban in outlook, and too disdainful of the benefits of prosperity and technology," and he calls, instead, for "an ethic of self-conscious material moderation . . . [that] requires neither a log cabin nor a hairshirt, but a deliberate ordering of priorities so as to distinguish between the necessary and superfluous, useful and wasteful, beautiful and vulgar."

Architecture and design generally should lead in this ethic of self-conscious material moderation. After all, good design begins with questions of what is necessary, useful, and beautiful in each situation and with each project, just as bad design often has superfluous, wasteful, and vulgar aspects to it. Where design has often failed us, and where it needs to lead us in the future, lies in its ability to temper the sheer quantity of material goods and sheer size of the physical environments that so many people have come to expect and see as normal. An ethic of material moderation needs to extend beyond the individual object or space, to encompass the amount of such things we think we need, as in architect Ross Chapin's designs for cottages in pocket neighborhoods.[9]

Figure 32.2 Conover Commons, Redmond, WA. Ross Chapin Architects. The Cottage Company developer. An ethic of material moderation needs to extend beyond the individual object or space, to encompass an entire community. Ross Chapin's designs for pocket neighborhoods reveal the richness possible, with very small "cottages" sharing ample outdoor community space.

This is counter to the idea that runs deep in Western culture, that each individual has the right to live as they see fit, even if that means living excessively and wastefully. As Shi acknowledges, "What meaningful simple living does require is a person willing it for himself. Attempts to impose simple living have been notoriously ephemeral in their effects. For simplicity to be both fulfilling and sustaining, one must choose it, or, as the Puritans might have said, one must be chosen for it."[10] But design plays a powerful role in what people will for themselves, and architects and designers have much more influence than often assumed.

Designer Philippe Starck, for example, envisioned a series of products for a major U.S. retailer in which every product, designed to have a very low cost, had another use built into it: a wastebasket that became a stool, a pen that became a light, etc. Starck has also said in lectures that while he has designed chairs that cost $100, his goal is to design a $1 chair, so inexpensive that every person on the planet could afford one.[11] Starck's approach shows the two-pronged way in which design can move us to a world based on material moderation. On one hand, designers can build multiple purposes and continual reuse into everything we do, so that people simply need fewer things in order to meet their daily needs. And on the other, designers can invert the unfortunate equation of design with costliness and, instead, make every design as absolutely inexpensive as possible.

The economist Robert Frank has shown how people will spend excessively in pursuit of status and feel deprived unless they, too, have what those whose status they aspire to also have, an endless upward spiral of empty aspiration that Frank calls "positional arms races."[12] The challenge—and opportunity—for architects and designers lies in using this search for status to reverse the spiral and have people aspire to having as little as possible and living as simply as possible, not by imposing it on them, but by helping them will it for themselves. This has happened before. The history of design shows how periods of excess—the Rococo period of the eighteenth century, the Victorian period of the nineteenth century—often precede periods of great restraint—Neo-Classicism, Modernism. Never have we needed an extended period of restraint more than now, and it may, once again, fall on the design community to help lead us to that place by making the question of what we can live without the question that everyone will now have to begin to live with.

33

The Adulthood of the Species

In *The Sociology of Intellectual Life*, sociologist Steve Fuller lays out an agenda for academics — and indeed, all professionals whose livelihood depends upon the discovery or application of knowledge — that pertains to the new demands we face as civilization and a species. "Intellectuals," writes Fuller, "differ from ordinary academics in holding that the truth is best approached not by producing new knowledge, but by destroying old beliefs . . . The intellectual's ethic is both exhilarating and harsh, for it places the responsibility for thinking squarely on the thinker's shoulders. Every act of deference thus becomes an abdication of one's own intellectual authority."[1] He goes on to argue that the overly deferential behavior of too many academics and professionals comes from being "rewarded for feats of ventriloquism, that is, an ability to speak through the authority of others. The result is institutionalized cowardice," epitomized in the design community by the effete architect and educator in Charles Dickens's novel *Martin Chuzzlewit* — Mr. Pecksniff — who never does anything that others haven't done before.[2]

While such over-cautiousness may not matter much in a period of stability and security, it becomes highly destabilizing in a time of rapid change and great flux such as now. The very intellectuals who should lead the way forward have too often become followers, suggests Fuller, having become too timid to take on the very institutions and professions that have granted the tenure or license that intellectuals supposedly need in order to speak out against the status quo. And just as ironically, the public has begun to question the need for the protections of tenure and licensure if those who benefit from it do not use it on behalf of the public interest. Why have such institutionalized protections if tenured academics or licensed professionals never put their position to the test by speaking out about issues that matter to the public and communicating in venues and in ways that the public will hear and understand?

Fuller gives a humorous, step-by-step guide on how to overcome the public stage fright of academics. The first step: "Whatever has already been said . . . whatever you do, don't say those things." And of the significant ideas that have not been said, "which ones come with a pretext likely to promote maximum exposure, participation, and impact? That's what you say." This process involves learning "how to improvise on the world-historic stage," as Fuller calls it, echoing Hegel, and how to "say what needs to be said in a situation where you are well positioned to say it."[3] Were we to follow that advice, what ideas seem most likely to have the greatest impact? Let me suggest two.

The first involves recognizing that we remain an immature species and that we will need to mature very quickly if we hope to survive into the adulthood of our species. This is not a new idea. The Native American Ojibway think of human beings as infants, dependent upon and responsible for the care of Mother Earth, relying, as children do parents, on other species, who can live quite well without us.[4] That idea underscores the hubris of humans putting ourselves at the peak of the pyramid of life, and the childishness of our exploitation and willful extinction of so many of the other species upon which we depend. And it clarifies the challenge we face: will we, as the children of this planet, grow up and learn to respect each other and our elders, as the Ojibway call other animals and plants, or will we, like tragically reckless youth, destroy what we most need in order to survive?

Our non-survival as a species seems so remote a possibility that we rarely raise it, in large part because we have convinced ourselves that our intelligence and technology have granted us a kind of invincibility. And yet, like careless teenagers careening down a hazardous road while believing they will live forever, the human species remains among the most vulnerable of all. Human societies have never been more globally interconnected and technologically efficient, and less resilient: less able to handle, physically and psychologically, the disruptive changes we will likely face as we encounter planetary tipping points in the decades ahead.

We already know where some of those tipping points lie: prolonged droughts that we cannot prevent, widespread crop failures we cannot stop, and global pandemics for which we have no cure. And we have seen how human communities can drive themselves into near extinction, as happened on Easter Island after the native population denuded the landscape, in part to erect their famous statues, and had no way of constructing the canoes they needed to fish and feed themselves.

It seems ironic, in light of this, that people spend so much time arguing about our origin as a species, people who have overwhelming evidence to back up Darwin's claim of our evolution from other species and people who see humanity resulting from intelligent design, based either in faith or in facts that don't seem to fit evolutionary theory.[5] A more productive debate would focus not on Darwin's idea of the origin of the species, but instead on another Darwinian idea: the survival of the species—our own.

We might well ask, for example: what adaptive benefit arises from our remarkable ability as humans to delude ourselves about our vulnerability as a species? Knowing full well that all other species depend on the right environmental conditions in order to survive, why do we hold to the illusion that we, of all species, can avoid that fact? And clearly comprehending the finite nature of the resources on this planet, why do we continue to act as if they were infinite and to hold to political ideologies and economic incentives that perpetuate our over-consumption of what we know cannot last? When, in short, will we rouse ourselves from our technologically induced and socially enforced stupor long enough to acknowledge the immaturity of our relationship with the planet and with each other, before we go the way of the dodo bird?

Reaching the adulthood of our species will demand that we leave our collective adolescence behind and grow up. This will entail self-sacrifice: consuming no more than what we absolutely need to live. It will demand delayed gratification: stewarding the resources we will need indefinitely to survive. And it will require service to others before ourselves: protecting all those who we depend on—be they other people or all the plant and animal populations with whom we share the planet—that future generations of humans will need to thrive. We know how to do this as individual adults, partners, parents, and friends, but we have yet to achieve this as a species, to put in place a human society in which justice and the good of others reign. And we have yet to speak the truth to all those who would call such sentiments childish or naive or who elevate greed, selfishness, or power as worthy ends. They are the true juveniles among us, too immature to see the self-destructiveness in what they espouse.

The adulthood of our species will also require that we see the connections among things often kept separate and thought of as distinct, resisting the temptation to reduce the world to established categories, fixed identities, or defined territories, while embracing the dynamic complexity, heterogeneity, and non-linearity that char-acterizes healthy ecosystems. Our maturation will also come with the recognition that what makes youth truly valuable is not the envy and selfishness around which we have built so much of our current economy and society, but instead the creativity, imagination, and openness to new experiences and to the construction of new identities.

No one likes to be called childish, least of all the children who like to pass for adults. For that reason, the maturing of the human species to the point where we can inhabit the planet with the same equanimity as all the other species we share it with will take real parenting skill. We may need to use some reverse psychology, not using words like "equity" or "sustainability" in some settings, since they tend to set off the teenage adults among us. And we may need to accept that bottom-up peer pressure will be more effective than top-down rules and regulations, which no one in the teenage of humanity will want to follow. Throughout it all, we will need to keep in mind the question that Gilles Deleuze and Felix Guattari so aptly asked, "Why do men fight for their servitude as stubbornly as though it were their salvation?"[6] Revealing the servitude that lies at the heart of humanity's unsustainable practices and exposing the almost Orwellian misuse of terms like "freedom" and "happiness" in our current global economy and political culture remains one of the most important tasks ahead of us, as we finally grow up as a species—and none too soon.

34

Media, Metaphor, and Meaning

Marshall McLuhan's well-known phrase, "the medium is the message" has taken on new meaning in our times.[1] Gutenberg's invention of movable type in the mid-fifteenth century led to profound changes in almost every aspect of modern culture, including the rise of the protestant reformation in the sixteenth century, the scientific revolution in the seventeenth century, the democratic revolutions in the eighteenth century, and the industrial revolution in the nineteenth century. It also helped give rise to the machine as a metaphor for reality. The mechanism of the printing press, in other words, helped spawn a conception of the world and everything in it as obeying mechanical laws and operating like a machine. That idea, while a powerful engine behind many of the innovations that have come to characterize the modern world, has also helped prompt the widely held presumption that we, as the makers of machines, have the right to treat the rest of reality as an extension of—and indeed, the very fuel for—the mechanisms we create for ourselves.

Such an idea remains so firmly embedded in the modern world that it will take a long time to change, as it took a long time for the medieval mindset to moderate in the wake of the machine metaphor. But change it will with the profound change in medium we have embarked upon. The digital revolution, as many have observed, constitutes not just an extension of the printed book that has existed since Gutenberg, but also a dramatic change in how we gather data, convey information, and share knowledge. And with it has come an equally dramatic shift in the dominant view of reality, moving from a mechanistic model to a biological one, from a machine-like to a web-like metaphor, from vertical hierarchies to networked systems.[2]

Unlike a machine, designed from the start and operated from above as a coordinated system, a web comprises a self-organizing, evolving set of relationships that resist outside control and that operate across myriad nodes and links with no single designer or operator. The worldwide web epitomizes that web-like structure, but so does the "web of life," as ecologists have come to call nature's ecosystems, and the social networks that social scientists see as fundamental to human communities.[3] That we still see mistaken efforts at top-down control on the part of leaders, misplaced notions of efficiency on the part of managers, and misunderstood conceptions of systems on the part of designers shows how resilient that unresilient way of thinking remains. But we have seen how much such thinking has undermined governments, destroyed companies, and fractured infrastructure, all signs that the several-hundred-year-old mechanistic metaphor has begun to fail us. And we have also seen enough of the success of socially mediated political campaigns, of entrepreneurial web-based businesses, and of invincible networks of like-minded advocates-for-a-cause to know how powerful this new metaphor can be. No one needs to impose it or decree it. As happened with the printed book, the digital web will prevail through its sheer ability to empower those left out of the previous reign.

This change in media and metaphor will also bring a change in methods, as happened in the wake of Gutenberg. For instance, a web-like world will likely see those forces that arose in the wake of the Enlightenment diminish, and less hierarchical and less clearly defined structures emerge. We may see the waning of competitive or adversarial relationships and the emerging of cooperative and collaborative ones, as the work of game theorists like John Nash has suggested;[4] the withering of national economies and the growing of metropolitan ones, as economic analysts such as Jane Jacobs have argued;[5] the weakening of literacy and the strengthening of visual culture, as the work of theorists such as Ivan Illich has asserted;[6] and the wasting away of expert-based authority and the rise of vernacular culture and the amateur, as cultural observers like Charles Leadbeater have posited.[7]

Changes in the meaning of what we do will also likely occur as a result of this shift. The modern world has focused on the creation of jobs, and developed public policies around having a job and helping those without jobs get them. And as economist Jeremy Rifkin has shown, we have entered a period characterized by the disappearance of jobs, which undermines the very idea of jobs as the basis for one's identity and meaning.[8] Instead, we seem headed to a time in which doing meaningful work will prevail over having a good-paying job. Jobs can disappear or dwindle, but there remains an almost infinite amount of work to do in the world, and as a result an almost infinite number of opportunities for people seeking personal satisfaction through service to others.

In the design fields, for example, the global economy has led to a dramatic decrease in the number of jobs, as computer tools have greatly increased the productivity of people and the geographical reach of professionals. At the same time, with billions of people poorly housed and unsafely situated, the amount of work for designers to do has grown enormously. This represents a turning point for the design professions akin to that faced by the health fields in the nineteenth century and the legal fields in the twentieth.

The legal profession's transformation in the twentieth century offers one way of thinking about this.[9] Prior to the Great Depression, legal education focused primarily on preparing lawyers for trying cases in court. But as the supply of trial lawyers outgrew the demand and as social and economic change brought new opportunities, there arose a new conception of the law—legal realism—that viewed the law as an interdisciplinary, value-laden, and socially consequential field. In its wake, legal education began to move away from the formal analysis of cases and the narrow focus on principles toward an emphasis on legal thinking and on the broad application of that thinking in the world. As a result, the legal profession has become involved (for better or worse) in almost all aspects of our lives, with many lawyers never setting foot in a courtroom.

Other fields, including the design professions, seem in the midst of a similar transformation. Since the 1960s and the rise of activism, professional education has expanded to embrace a wide range of once-radical activities, including critical theory, community participation, evidence-based decision-making, integrated practice, environment-behavior research, and sustainability studies, among many others.[10] Like legal realism, these diverse areas of investigation sometimes seem at odds with each other, but they all share a realist commitment to addressing social, environmental, and economic inequities and to changing rather than simply embellishing the world as it is.

This expansion of purview does not negate the value of traditional professional education. Just as law schools still produce trial lawyers, so too will those in other fields like design still educate students to practice in ways that serve fee-paying clients. But the shift in approach that happened in legal education in the twentieth century will — and has already begun to — occur in most other professions in the twenty-first, in response to the overwhelming disparity between the demands of billions of people in need and the supply of professionals able to address those needs.

As happened with legal realism, this shift will likely lead to a more interdisciplinary form of education, preparing graduates for much wider applications of their knowledge. On one hand, that may prompt a new emphasis on epistemology — on how we think — and a de-emphasis on defining our fields according to the traditional results of practice. On the other hand, this shift may lead to more specialization, based not on conventional categories, but on the changing nature of people's needs and the problems they face. Both of these trends — the broader application and narrower specialization of knowledge — will, in turn, demand a greater emphasis on research in professional fields like design. Understanding the nature of the needs of people and the planet and the most appropriate and resilient response to them will become paramount as we go through challenging and sometimes catastrophic changes in the century ahead of us.

35

The Nature of Things to Come

As we have seen throughout this book, the fracture-critical nature of the world that we have constructed and the more resilient future that we need to create both revolve around the question of scale. It may seem from the discussion so far that large-scale systems remain inherently vulnerable to catastrophic collapse and that small-scale systems can resist such consequences, or at least prevent a collapse from affecting a large number of people. But the real problem lies in the disjunction between the scale of our thinking and our action. Most fracture-critical systems and structures represent large-scale actions arising from small-scale thinking—from looking at the shortest paybacks, the narrowest benefits, and the most immediate returns to those with the most invested. "The essential problem," wrote historian Alfred Zimmern, "is how to govern a large-scale world with small-scale local minds."[1]

We cannot change the scale of the world, but we can change the scale of our thinking about it. As the sociologist of disasters Enrico Quarantelli has compellingly argued, disasters are fundamentally social events that not only disrupt and alter human activities and relationships, but also arise out of how we construct the physical world.[2] Natural events like tremors, hurricanes, or volcanoes do not constitute disasters until we have made ourselves vulnerable to their effects, according to where we situate and how we accommodate ourselves. As the saying goes, "Earthquakes don't kill people. Buildings do."

Why we continue to put ourselves in harm's way may have a lot to do with what sociologist Lee Clarke describes as "probabilist" as opposed to "possibilist" thinking.[3] Many of those in positions of power and authority tend to be probabilists when it comes to disasters, argues Clarke, accepting a high degree of risk because of the benefits it can accrue for the very elites doing the disaster planning. The stressing of systems to the point of collapse exemplifies this behavior. Business and political elites often have much to gain and little to lose on the way up the exponential stress curves we have seen, while everyone else has the most to lose on the rapid descent once rupture occurs. Clarke calls, instead, for "possibilist" thinking, imagining the worst that can happen and realistically planning for that. Such "possibilist" thinking underpins this book and links disaster planning to design thinking: the iterative and participatory process of imagining future scenarios and critiquing them according to all that could possibly go wrong or fail to perform as expected.

Design thinking also involves getting things in their correct scale, and accounting for possible problems at all scales. Too much disaster planning produces what Clarke calls "fantasy documents," that often propose either overly simplistic solutions—assuming that everyone could evacuate New Orleans by car in the event of a levee break, for example—or overly complex ones—having so many emergency systems and procedures on the Deepwater Horizon, for instance, that no one knew how to proceed prior to the BP oil spill. The same fracture-critical thinking that led to these disasters, in other words, too often underpins our response to them, recalling the observation of Albert Einstein that "We can't solve problems by using the same kind of thinking we used when we created them."[4]

Resilient thinking, like design thinking when done well, ensures that the best possible solution to a problem has the appropriate degree of complexity at the proper scale, while assessing effects at a range of other scales, both smaller and larger than the one the problem seems to involve. Just as New Orleans needed a much more redundant levee system, with many more layers and easily containable compartments in the case of a break, so too did New

Orleans need a much more robust evacuation system, with many more modes of transporting people to safety and places of refuge for those who could not escape. At the same time, the larger-scale destruction of Louisiana's delta wetlands and the smaller-scale destruction of community in some of New Orleans's more impoverished areas both had direct bearing not only on the levee system's ability to protect people, but also on the city's ability to evacuate people. Disaster response, like a good design response, considers possible consequences at a number of scales and the impacts of systems that may seem unrelated to the problem at hand.

And, going forward, good design and planning should start with the assumption that nothing will work as intended—or even at all.[5] We should, in other words, take nothing for granted and act as if we have only those within our community and that within our control to depend on. That may seem excessively alarmist or pessimistic, but it is, in fact, the only way to avoid the true alarm of being a victim of a catastrophic failure that we never saw coming and over which we have no control. And it is the only way to achieve the real optimism of knowing that we can survive, and indeed thrive, regardless of what may happen. We are at our best when we have imagined and accounted for the worst.

This ultimate principle of resilient design has several consequences. First, it unleashes the creativity, commitment, and community that seem to arise among groups of people as they deal with the aftermath of a catastrophe. As author Rebecca Solnit has documented in *A Paradise Built in Hell*, disasters, "demonstrate what is possible or, perhaps more accurately, latent: the resilience and generosity of those around us and their ability to improvise another kind of society. Second, they demonstrate how deeply most of us desire connection, participation, altruism, and purposefulness."[6] Solnit's analysis also shows how the elites of society, "hierarchies and institutions . . . are often what fails in such crises. Civil society is what succeeds, not only in an emotional demonstration of altruism and mutual aid but also in a practical mustering of creativity and resources to meet the challenges."

Second, the principle of taking nothing for granted underscores the need for, and indeed the efficiency of, providing multiple independent and redundant ways of doing things. This may sound inefficient or not cost effective, but history proves just the opposite. Humans have, for most of our history, created our world this way, built with what we had readily available and easily attainable, fueled by renewable resources that we could repeatedly harvest without diminishing them for future generations, and conceived of as multi-functional and quickly adaptable to the unforeseen circumstances that await us. We have come to see those older ways of living as primitive or impoverished. But we need to see the work of our ancestors anew, not as more rudimentary than our own, but quite the contrary as more resilient and resourceful, and more flexible and dependable than the extremely fragile, fracture-critical world that we have since created.

Finally, the principle of taking nothing for granted gives back to people the possibility of achieving true happiness. This may sound presumptive and even paradoxical given the unhappiness that often precedes and surely follows a disaster, but true happiness, according to the Roman stoics who lived in a time of serial catastrophes much like our own, lies in attending to that over which we have control: ourselves.[7] Everything else, according to the stoics, lies beyond our control and so has no effect on our happiness. While seemingly austere or harsh, such stoicism offers not only a way for individuals to retain a sense of hope and even a sense of humor in a fracture-critical world, but also a practical way of withstanding whatever disaster may descend upon us.

As a design strategy, stoicism also gives us a very resilient way to proceed. Just as stoics urged people to imagine the very worst that could happen in order to prepare them for it and to help them appreciate the present, so too should we design the world as if the worst will happen. In such a thought experiment, we might begin by asking: what could possibly occur in any given situation and how would we deal with it, both physically and psychologically? How would we live, for example, in a world without affordable oil or available electricity, without global communications or transcontinental travel, without plentiful food or accessible water, without personal safety or political stability, without a secure income or a sure job?

Most of us, of course, don't want to think of such things, and hope that we never have to, even though we know that billions of people on the planet face some or all of those conditions every day. But, as philosopher John Rawls helped us see, we all live behind what he called the "veil of ignorance," unsure what our future holds and whether or not we will continue to have what we now do, going forward.[8] Rawls argued that, as a result, every action we take should ensure that the least fortunate among us should benefit from whatever we do, since we may well be that person now or in the future. The same argument applies to the design of our world. We should assume that whatever we have now may not last and that whatever we assume is now available may not be so someday soon.

That ethic seems as far as it could be from that which underlies much of the modern world. As Solnit describes it, "Mobile and individualistic modern societies [argue that] . . . we are essentially selfish, and because you will not care for me, I cannot care for you. I will not feed you because I must hoard against starvation, since I too cannot count on others. Better yet, I will take your wealth and add it to mine—if I believe that my well-being is independent of yours or pitted against yours—and justify my conduct as natural law . . . Thus does everyday life become a social disaster."[9] The irony in such an argument lies in using the possibility of disaster to create the true disaster of everyone for themselves and everyone else be damned.

The idea of modern societies as social disasters—slow-motion disasters—comes from the mistaken belief that we can control other people—"Better yet, I will take your wealth"—and other species—"I must hoard against starvation." This makes the fundamental error, as stoicism and indeed almost every religion has long recognized, of thinking we can control what isn't under our control, while missing the point that we can only control ourselves. Such self-control leads not to selfishness, but just the opposite: requiring very little, wanting nothing more, and stewarding whatever we have. That may sound like impoverishment to those who have become accustomed to needing a lot, wanting too much, and wasting much of what we have, but such values, which have helped fuel the exponentially stressed systems, structures, and environments that we depend on, also leave us completely unprepared for the consequences of their collapse.

36

Hell or Paradise?

After studying people's behavior in the wake of five major catastrophes, Solnit shows that "the prevalent human nature in disaster is resilient, resourceful, generous, empathic, and brave." She concludes that "Disaster reveals what else the world could be like . . . reveals mutual aid as a default operating principle and civil society as something waiting in the wings when it's absent from the stage . . . The task before us is to recognize the possibilities visible through that gateway and endeavor to bring them in to the realm of the everyday."[1] Resiliency, in other words, lies latently in each one of us and is unleashed during and immediately after a disaster. The question that Solnit raises, though, is how to bring that into our everyday lives, how to cultivate resourceful resiliency as a valued trait, stoic self-control as an admired virtue, and unreciprocated generosity as a social norm. This may sound utopian—"the brief utopias that flash up in disaster," as Solnit puts it—but such characteristics will soon become all too real and present in our lives, as we stand here, at the dawn of the twenty-first century, and look ahead to a fracture-critical future full of the disasters we have designed for ourselves. Call it, as Solnit does, "a paradise built in hell," but whether it turns out to be paradise or simply hell depends upon how constructively, creatively, and selflessly we respond.

What might "paradise" look like? First, it would align the scales of event, thinking, and action so that for large-scale problems we would engage in large-scale thinking about possible solutions. For example, a climate-change or disease-driven collapse of our global food system, as large scale a problem as we might imagine, would require that we think in large-scale terms about the social and environmental effects of feeding the human population. The local foods movement, in that sense, involves not just a small-scale solution to a very big problem, but also a large-scale way of thinking about how we can nourish some seven billion people in an environmentally responsible and socially resilient way. Hell comes from small-minded responses to big problems; paradise, from thinking as broad as the problem itself.

At the same time, small-scale problems require small-scale solutions, attuned to the needs of particular populations and places on the planet. Rather than seek large-scale, universal solutions to local problems, we need to enable people at the smallest and most immediate scale possible to find resolutions that fit their needs and capacities. The "extraordinary communities" that Solnit found arising in response to disasters almost always occurred in a spontaneous, participatory, and ad hoc way, and lasted only as long as required to do the work that had to be done.[2] We cannot plan such communities, which is precisely the point. Instead, we must find ways to allow them to happen, ideally not just after a disaster but as a way to prevent disasters from occurring in the first place, and of enabling people to form the bonds and to practice the mutual aid that will ensure their survival regardless of the situation they face.

A second feature of "paradise" draws on the first: encouraging webs of alliances and networks of allegiances among people to flourish. As Bill McKibben argues in his book *Eaarth*, we have waited too long to stem the changes we have wrought to our planet, and so our main task now involves preparing ourselves for the worst, building up our local reserves and human resources, while scaling back on our expectations of wealth and exploitation of natural resources.[3] McKibben, though, also sees the Internet and its potential for global understanding and information sharing as the one innovation of our time worth preserving and extending. We need, in other words, to build local webs and the world wide web at the same time, and to see them as a continuous, resilient system across scales.

That leads to a third feature of the likely future in front of us: learning to live within our ecological footprint as a species. To understand what that means, consider the following two equations. The one, based on physics, has come to represent the twentieth century: Einstein's $E = mc^2$. Encapsulating the relationship of matter and energy, that equation also epitomizes the last century's pursuit of power, speed, and acceleration, which has helped fuel some of the exponential increases we have traced here. The other equation, based on biology, may come to represent the twenty-first century: $E = m^{\frac{3}{4}}$. As Geoffrey West describes it, "the metabolic rate varies as mass raised to the ¾ . . . man is a little less than 100 watts in metabolism (a light bulb)—that's about 2000 calories a day."[4]

That relationship seems to apply to all animal species, with the exception of humans, whose use of technology has massively increased our absorption of energy, with each person now having the metabolism equivalent, according to West, greater than that of a blue whale.

How much energy does our lifestyle [in America] require? Well, when you add up all our calories and then you add up the energy needed to run the computer and the air-conditioner, you get an incredibly large number, somewhere around 11,000 watts. Now you can ask yourself: What kind of animal requires 11,000 watts to live? And what you find is that we have created a lifestyle where we need more watts than a blue whale. We require more energy than the biggest animal that has ever existed. That is why our lifestyle is unsustainable. We can't have seven billion blue whales on this planet. It's not even clear that we can afford to have 300 million blue whales.[5]

The great challenge of our time entails reducing the average human energy requirement by a factor of 110, from 11,000 watts per person to 100 watts. That may seem impossible, but only if we assume that the last hundred years—one-thousandth of our existence as a

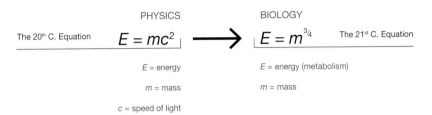

PHYSICS

The 20ᵗʰ C. Equation $E = mc^2$

E = energy

m = mass

c = speed of light

BIOLOGY

$E = m^{3/4}$ The 21ˢᵗ C. Equation

E = energy (metabolism)

m = mass

Figure 36.1 Just as Einstein's $E = mc^2$ epitomized the last century, the equation $E = m^{3/4}$ (metabolic rate equals mass raised to the ¾ power) may epitomize the twenty-first century.

species—is the norm and all the rest of our history, an aberration. Once we realize that humans long thrived on 100 watts a day, we can begin to imagine such a world again in the future, one in which people use tools rather than machines, muscle power rather than nuclear power, renewable rather than non-renewable resources, and food rather than the remains of fossils as fuel.

Doing so leads us to a fourth and final feature of a possible paradise: rediscovering what we once knew. "The age of missing information," as Bill McKibben called it in his book by that name[6] has created the paradoxical situation of our having more information than humans have ever had in our history, and at the same time, more missing information than ever before. We have fooled ourselves into thinking that we know more and are better off than those who came before us, but we have confused the appearance of a more primitive existence by our ancestors with the reality that they mostly lived richer and more resilient lives than most of us do now. As McKibben writes, "We . . . live at a moment of deep ignorance, when vital knowledge that humans have always possessed about who we are and where we live seems beyond our reach. An Un-enlightenment. An age of missing information."

The task before us amounts to relinquishing our attachment to the unhealthy and unsustainable path we have wandered down over the last two centuries and returning to the path we have long been on as a species, remembering what we once knew, and relishing the wealth, now so often overlooked, of all that is free and in infinite supply: family and friends, love and learning, cultivation and co-creation. In such relationships and activities lies our real resiliency as individuals and sustainability as a species. And to imagine what such a world, built on such principles, would be like, we have only to look at what our ancestors have left behind for us and at what our progeny would undoubtedly want us to leave behind for them. Let's begin.

Notes

Preface: Designed Catastrophes

1 Tabuchi, Hiroko, Sanger, David E., and Bradsher, Keith. "Japan Faces Potential Nuclear Disaster as Radiation Levels Rise," *New York Times*. March 14, 2011. www.nytimes.com/2011/03/15/world/asia/15nuclear.html

2 Bastrow, David Rohde, and Saul, Stephanie. "Deepwater Horizon's Final Hours," *New York Times*. December 25, 2010. www.nytimes.com/2010/12/26/us/26spill.html

3 "The World Needs to Draw the Lessons of Hurricane Katrina," UN/ISDR. August 29, 2006. www.unisdr.org/archive/5407

4 Romero, Simon, and Lacey, Marc. "Fierce Quake Devastates Haitian Capital," *New York Times*. January 12, 2010. www.nytimes.com/2010/01/13/world/americas/13haiti.html

5 Benedictow, Ole J. *The Black Death 1346–1353: The Complete History*. Woodbridge, UK: Boydell Press, 2004. Russell Thornton. "Aboriginal North American Population and Rates of Decline, ca. A.D. 1500–1900," *Current Anthropology*, vol. 38, no. 2 (April, 1997): 310–315.

6 "What Killed the Dinosaurs?" Public Broadcasting System, WGBH, Boston. www.pbs.org/wgbh/evolution/extinction/dinosaurs/

7 Sorkin, Andrew Ross. "Lehman Files for Bankruptcy; Merrill Is Sold," *New York Times*. September 14, 2008. www.nytimes.com/2008/09/15/business/15lehman.html?pagewanted=all

8 Green, Steve. "Report: Nearly 70 Percent of LV Homeowners Underwater on Mortgage," *Las Vegas Sun*. November 30, 2009. www.lasvegassun.com/news/2009/nov/30/report-nearly-70-percent-lv-home owners-underwater-/ "2010 Foreclosures in Minnesota: A Report Based on County Sheriff's Sale Data," Minnesota Home Ownership Center, Greater Minnesota Housing Fund, Minnesota Housing Finance Agency, Family Housing Fund. February 9, 2011. www.gmhf.com

1 The Increasing Incidence of Disasters

1   International Strategy for Disaster Reduction, United Nations (UNISDR), www.unisdr.org/
2   Ibid.
3   Quoted from a talk delivered at the Association of Collegiate Schools of Architecture administrator's conference, "Preparing for the Inconvenient Truth," November 1–3, 2007. Minneapolis, Minnesota.
4   UNISDR. www.unisdr.org/
5   Ibid.
6   "Countries and National Platforms," UNISDR. www.unisdr.org/partners/countries
7   Ibid.
8   Below, Regina, Wirtz Angelica and Guha-Sapir, Debarati. "Disaster Category Classification and Peril Terminology for Operational Purposes," Centre for Research on the Epidemiology of Disease (CRED). http://cred.be/sites/default/files/DisCatClass_264.pdf
9   "Worldwide Weather and Climate Events," National Climate Data Center, Department of Commerce. http://lwf.ncdc.noaa.gov/oa/reports/weather-events.html
10 "International Data Base, World Population Summary." U.S. Census Bureau. www.census.gov/population/international/data/idb/worldpopinfo.php
11 Williams, Rob, Gero, Shane, Bejder, Lars, Calambokidis, John, Kraus, Scott D., Lusseau, David, Read, Andrew J., and Robbins, Jooke. "Underestimating the Damage: Interpreting Cetacean Carcass Recoveries in the Context of the *Deepwater Horizon*/BP incident," *Conservation Letters.* March 30, 2011. onlinelibrary.wiley.com/doi/10.1111/j.1755-263X.2011.00168.x/abstract

2 Our Planetary Ponzi Scheme

1   Barash, David. "We Are All Madoffs," *The Chronicle Review.* August 31, 2009. http://chronicle.com/article/We-Are-All-Madoffs/48182/
2   Ibid.
3   Morales, Evo. "Capitalism is the Worst Enemy of Humanity," speech to the United Nations meeting on climate change. September 24, 2007. http://climateandcapitalism.com/?p=210
4   Barash. "We Are All Madoffs."
5   "World Footprint: Do We Fit on the Planet?" *Global Footprint Network.* www.footprintnetwork.org/en/index.php/GFN/page/world_footprint/
6   Barash. "We Are All Madoffs."
7   "Pascal's Wager," *Stanford Encyclopedia of Philosophy.* June 4, 2008. http://plato.stanford.edu/entries/pascal-wager/

3 Fracture-Critical Design

1   "Interstate 35W Bridge in Minneapolis," Minnesota Department of Transportation. www.dot.state.mn.us/i35wbridge/
2   Ibid.
3   Gunderson, Lance H., and Holling, C.S. *Panarchy: Understanding Transformations in Human and Natural Systems.* Washington D.C.: Island Press, 2002.

4 Disasters on Demand

1   Klein, Naomi. *The Shock Doctrine: The Rise of Disaster Capitalism.* New York: Henry Holt, 2007.
2   Ibid.
3   Schaeffer, Emily C., and Kashdan, Andrew. "Earth, Wind, and Fire! Federalism and Incentive in Natural Disaster Response," emilyskarbek. com/uploads/Chapter_10_-_Schaeffer_-_Final_Page_Proofs.pdf.
4   Reinert, Hugo, and Reinert, Erik. "Creative Destruction in Economics: Nietzsche, Sombart, Schumpeter," www.springerlink.com/content/j0g 1348m35327v04/
5   Klein. *The Shock Doctrine.*
6   Ueckert, Steve. "The Fall of Enron," *Houston Chronicle.* www.chron.com/ news/specials/enron/

5 The Anti-Shock Doctrine

1   DeWall, Nathan, and Baumeister, Roy. "From Terror to Joy: Automatic Tuning to Positive Affective Information Following Mortality Salience," *Psychological Science*, vol. 18 (2007): 984–990.
2   Saulny, Susan. "In New Orleans, It's a Cram Course in Public Service 101," *New York Times.* September 6, 2006, www.nytimes.com/2006/ 09/06/education/06education.html?ref=hurricanekatrina Banerjee, Neela. "In New Orleans, Rebuilding With Faith," *New York Times.* October 26, 2007. www.nytimes.com/2007/10/26/us/26churches.html
3   "Engagement with the World," Designmatters, Art Center College of Design. http://www.artcenter.edu/designmatters
4   "The Los Angeles Earthquake: Get Ready," January 2008, Art Center College of Design.
5   "The 2030 Challenge," *Architecture 2030.* www.architecture2030.org/
6   Wolgast, Elizabeth. *Ethics of an Artificial Person: Lost Responsibility in Professions and Organizations.* Palo Alto: Stanford University Press, 1992.
7   Klein. *The Shock Doctrine.*

6 Redefining Success

1   Dramstad, Wenche E., Olson, James D., and Forman, Richard T.T. *Landscape Ecology Principles in Landscape Architecture and Land-Use Planning.* Cambridge, MA: Harvard University Press, 1996.

2   McLuhan, Marshall, and Powers, Bruce R. *The Global Village: Transformations in World Life and Media in the 21ˢᵗ Century.* Oxford: Oxford University Press, 1989.

3   Putnam, Robert D. *Bowling Alone: The Collapse and Revival of American Community.* New York: Simon & Schuster, 2000.

4   Based on a study of the early automobile industry in Cleveland, Ohio, which I wrote for the Historic American Engineering Record, U.S. Department of Interior in 1979. Available online http://lcweb2.loc. gov/pnp/habshaer/oh/oh0100/oh0117/data/oh0117data.pdf

5   Ingrassia, Paul. *Crash Course: The American Automobile Industry's Road from Glory to Disaster.* New York: Random House, 2010.

6   Sorkin, Andrew Ross. *Too Big to Fail: The Inside Story of How Wall Street and Washington Fought to Save the Financial System – and Themselves.* New York: Penguin Books, 2009.

7   Frank, Robert, and Cook, Philip J. *The Winner-Take-All Society: Why the Few at the Top Get So Much More Than the Rest of Us.* New York: Penguin Books, 1995.

8   McDonough, William, and Braungart, Michael. *Cradle to Cradle: Remaking the Way We Make Things.* New York: North Point Press, 2002.

7 Fracture-Critical Species

1   Crutzen, Paul J. and Schwägerl, Christian. "Living in the Anthropocene: Toward a New Global Ethos," *Environment 360.* January 24, 2011. http://e360.yale.edu/feature/living_in_the_anthropocene_toward_a_new _global_ethos/2363/

2   Diamond, Jared. *Collapse: How Societies Choose to Fail or Succeed.* New York: Viking, 2005.

3   Femmer, Randolph. *What Every Citizen Should Know About Our Planet.* Oak Hill, FL: M. Arman Publishing, 2011.

4   Ibid.

5   Simon, Julian. *Hoodwinking the Nation.* New Brunswick, NJ: Transaction, 1999.

6   Shiva, Vandana. *The Violence of the Green Revolution: Third World Agriculture, Ecology, and Politics.* New York: Zed Books, 2000.

7   Diamond. *Collapse.*

8 Re-sizing the Human Footprint

1   Moran, Daniel D., Wackernagel, Mathis, Kitzes, Justin A., Goldfinger, Steven H., and Boutaud, Aurelien. "Measuring Sustainable Development

— Nation by Nation." *Ecological Economics*, vol. 64, no. 3 (January 15, 2008): 470–474. www.sciencedirect.com, www.elsevier.com/locate/ecolecon

2   "Ecological Creditors and Debtors," Global Footprint Network, www. footprintnetwork.org

3   Moran et al. "Measuring Sustainable Development."

4   Leinberger, Christopher. "The Next Slum?" *The Atlantic*. March 2008.

9 Fracture-Critical Population

1   Manaugh, Geoff, and Twilley, Nicola. "Landscapes of Quarantine," Storefront for Art and Architecture, New York, March 10–April 24, 2010. www.storefrontnews.org/exhibitions_events/exhibitions?e=170

2   Ibid.

3   Ibid.

4   Johnson, Steven. *The Ghost Map: The Story of London's Most Terrifying Epidemic – and How it Changed Science, Cities, and the Modern World.* London: Penguin Books, 2006

5   Manaugh, and Twilley "Landscapes of Quarantine."

6   "Pandemic (H1N1) 2009," *Global Alert and Response*. World Health Organization. www.who.int/csr/disease/swineflu/en/index.html

7   "Ebola hemorrhagic fever," *Global Alert and Response*. World Health Organization. www.who.int/csr/disease/ebola/en/index.html

8   McLuhan, Marshall. *The Gutenberg Galaxy: The Making of Typographic Man.* Toronto: University of Toronto Press, 1962.

9   Dawkins, Richard. *The Selfish Gene.* Oxford: Oxford University Press, 1976.

10 Hofstadter, Douglas. *Metamagical Themas: Questing for the Essence of Mind and Pattern.* New York: Basic Books, 1996.

10 Protective Design

1   Faller, Jim. "10 Ways to Protect Yourself from Computer Viruses." http://computers.6ln.com

2   Davis, Mike. *The Monster at our Door: The Global Threat of Avian Flu.* New York: Henry Holt, 2005

3   Davis, Mike. *Planet of Slums.* New York: Verso, 2006.

4   Meltzer, Martin I., Cox, Nancy J., and Fukuda, Keiji. "The Economic Impact of Pandemic Influenza in the United States: Priorities for Intervention," *Emerging Infectious Diseases*. Atlanta: Centers for Disease Control and Prevention. http://www.cdc.gov/ncidod/eid/vol5no5/meltzer.htm

5   Buckley, Robert M., and Kalarickal, Jerry (eds.). "Thirty Years of World Bank Shelter Lending: What Have We Learned?" Washington D.C.: The World Bank, 2006.

6   Mangili, Alexandra, and Gendreau, Mark A. "The Transmission of Infectious Diseases During Commercial Air Travel," *The Lancet*, vol. 365

(2005): 989–996. https://www.pall.com/pdf/Transmission_of_infectious_
diseases_during_commercial_air_travel.pdf

7   Khan, Kamran, Arino, Julien, Hu, Wei, Raposo, Paulo, Sears, Jennifer,
Calderon, Felipe, Heidebrecht, Christine, Macdonald, Michael, Liauw,
Jessica, Chan, Angie, and Gardam, Michael. "Spread of a Novel Influenza
A (H1N1) Virus via Global Airline Transportation," *The New England
Journal of Medicine*, vol. 361, no. 2 (July 9, 2009): 212–214.
http://content.nejm.org/cgi/content/full/NEJMc0904559

8   Valsecchi, M. "Mass Plague Graves Found On Venice 'Quarantine'
Island," *National Geographic*. August, 29, 2007.

9   Seitz, Sharon, and Miller, Stuart. *The Other Islands of New York City*.
Woodstock, VT: Countryman Press, 2003.

10 "Influenza 1918," *The American Experience*, Public Broadcasting System,
http://www.pbs.org/wgbh/americanexperience/films/influenza/player/

11 "Health Screening at Airports," http://www.pandemicflu.gov/individual
family/travelers/index.html#screen

12 Brownlee, Shannon, and Lenzer, Jeanne. "Does the Vaccine Matter?" *The
Atlantic*. November 2009.

13 Defoe, Daniel. *A Journal of the Plague Year*. Boston: D. Estes & Co., 1904.

14 Person, Bobbie, Sy, Francisco, Holton, Kelly, Govert, Barbara, Liang,
Arthur, and The NCID/SARS Community Outreach Team. "Fear and
Stigma: The Epidemic within the SARS Outbreak," *Emerging Infectious
Disease*. Atlanta: Centers for Disease Control, February 2004. http://
www.cdc.gov/ncidod/EID/vol10no2/03–0750.htm

15 Westfall, Richard S. *The Life of Isaac Newton*. Cambridge: Cambridge
University Press, 1994.

16 Kanaracus, Chris. "Telecommuting: A Quarter of U.S. Workers Do It
Regularly," *PC World*. IDG News Service, November 27, 2007. http://
www.pcworld.com/article/140003/telecommuting_a_quarter_of_us_
workers_do_it_regularly.html

17 Epstein, Paul. "Climate Change and Infectious Disease: Stormy Weather
Ahead?" *Epidemiology*, vol. 13, no. 4 (July 2002).

11 Fracture-Critical Economy

1   Chandra, Shobhana. "Recession in U.S. Was Even Worse Than
Estimated, Revisions Show," *Bloomberg*. July 30, 2010. www.bloomberg.
com/news/2010–07–30/recession-in-america-was-even-worse-than-
estimated-revisions-to-data-show.html

2   Smith, Donna. "U.S. Debt to Rise to $19.6 Trillion by 2015," *Reuters*.
June 8, 2010. www.reuters.com/article/2010/06/08/usa-treasury-debt-
idUSN088462520100608

3   Synnott, Thomas W. "The Debt Explosion of the 1980s: Problem and
Opportunity – Debt Ratio in the United State," *Moneywatch.com*. January
1991. http://findarticles.com/p/articles/mi_m1094/is_n1_v26/ai_9348064/

4   Leonhardt, David. "We're Spent," *New York Times*. July 17, 2011.
www.nytimes.com/2011/07/17/sunday-review/17economic.html

5   de la Merced, Michael J., Bajaj, Vikas, and Sorkin, Andrew Ross. "As Goldman and Morgan Shift, a Wall Street Era Ends." *New York Times.* September 21, 2008. http://dealbook.nytimes.com/2008/09/21/goldman-morgan-to-become-bank-holding-companies/

6   "Lehman Brothers Holdings Inc." *New York Times.* December 21, 2010. http://topics.nytimes.com/top/news/business/companies/lehman_brothers_holdings_inc/index.html

7   Labaton, Stephen. "S.E.C. Concedes Oversight Flaws Fueled Collapse." *New York Times.* September 26, 2008. www.nytimes.com/2008/09/27/business/27sec.html

8   Dudley, William C. "Regulatory Reform of the Global Financial System." Speech delivered at the Institute of Regulation & Risk North Asia, Hong Kong, April 12, 2011. www.newyorkfed.org/newsevents/speeches/2011/dud110412.html

12 Rethinking Work

1   Calabria, Mark A. "Dodd's Job-Killer." *New York Post.* April 20, 2010. www.cato.org/pub_display.php?pub_id=11707

2   Frank, Thomas. *What's the Matter with Kansas? How Conservatives Won the Heart of America.* New York: Metropolitan Books, 2004.

3   Borosage, Robert. "The Grip of the Old Economy." *Campaign for America's Future.* July 7, 2010.

4   Ibid.

5   These observations come from my conversations with and observations of the work of recent graduates from the College of Design at the University of Minnesota, an admittedly small sample, but one that I think reflects the thinking of a lot of young people today.

6   Arendt, Hannah. *The Human Condition.* Chicago: University of Chicago Press, 1958.

7   Ibid.

8   Rifkin, Jeremy. *The End of Work: The Decline of the Global Labor Force and the Dawn of the Post-Market Era.* New York: Putnam Books, 1995.

9   Ibid.

10   Morris, William. *News from Nowhere and Other Writings.* London: Penguin Books, 1993.

11   Ibid.

12   Ibid.

13   "Despite Recession, U.S. Entrepreneurial Activity Rises in 2009 to Highest Rate in 14 Year, Kauffman Study Shows," Ewing Marion Kauffman Foundation. May 20, 2010. www.kauffman.org/newsroom/despite-recession-us-entrepreneurial-activity-rate-rises-in-2009.aspx

13 Fracture-Critical Politics

1   McCarty, Nolan, Poole, Keith T., and Rosenthal, Howard. *Polarized America: The Dance of Ideology and Unequal Riches*. Boston: MIT Press, 2006.
2   Noah, Timothy. "The United States of Inequality," *Slate*. 10-part series running from September 3 to September 16, 2010. www.slate.com/id/2266025/entry/2266026/
3   "Smithsonian Magazine/Pew Research Poll about the Future Finds Widespread Optimism Despite Worries." June 24, 2010. http://news desk.si.edu/releases/smithsonian-magazinepew-research-poll-about-future-finds-widespread-optimism-despite-worries
4   Galbraith, John Kenneth. *The Affluent Society*. New York: Houghton Mifflin, 1998.
5   Beinart, Peter. *The Icarus Syndrome: A History of American Hubris*. Melbourne: Melbourne University Press, 2010.
6   Prestowitz, Clyde. *The Betrayal of American Prosperity: Free Market Delusions, America's Decline, and How We Must Compete in the Post-Dollar Era*. New York: Free Press, 2010.
7   "Distribution of Family Income – Gini Index," *The World Factbook*. Washington D.C.: Central Intelligence Agency. www.cia.gov/library/publications/the-world-factbook/fields/2172.html

14 Reimagining Government

1   Autry, James A., and Mitchell, Stephen. *Real Power: Business Lessons from the Tao Te Ching*. New York: Riverhead Books, 1998.
2   Rapport, David J., Lasley, William L., Rolston, Dennis E., Nielsen, N. Ole, Qualset, Calvin O., and Damania, Ardeshir B. *Managing for Healthy Ecosystems*. Boca Raton, FL: CRC Press, 2003.
3   Silver, Nate. "G.O.P.'s No-Tax Stance Is Outside Political Mainstream," *New York Times*. July 13, 2011. http://fivethirtyeight.blogs.nytimes.com/2011/07/13/house-republicans-no-tax-stance-far-outside-political-mainstream/
4   Dugatkin, Lee Alan. *Cooperation among Animals: An Evolutionary Perspective*. Oxford: Oxford University Press, 1997.
5   Bourdieu, Pierre. "The forms of capital," *Handbook of Theory and Research for the Sociology of Education*. New York: Greenwood, 1986, pp. 241–258.
6   Schalansky, Judith. *Atlas of Remote Islands*. New York: Penguin Books, 2010.
7   Illich, Ivan. *Tools for Conviviality*. New York: Harper & Row, 1973.

15 Fracture-Critical Higher Education

1   *The Chronicle of Higher Education*. http://chronicle.com
2   Hofstadter, Richard. *Anti-Intellectualism in American Life*. New York: Vintage Books, 1962.

3   "The Truth About Denial," *Newsweek*, August 2007. www.newsweek. com/2007/08/13/the-truth-about-denial.html "Federal Debt Limit (Debt Ceiling) & Deficit Talks," *New York Times*, July 21, 2011. http://topics.ny times.com/topics/reference/timestopics/subjects/n/national_debt_us/in dex.html

4   Gabriel, Trip. "Teachers Wonder, Why the Scorn?" *New York Times*. March 2, 2011. www.nytimes.com/2011/03/03/education/03teacher.html

5   Dillon, John. *The Heirs of Plato: A Study of the Old Academy*. Oxford: Oxford University Press, 2003.

6   Krause, Elliott. *The Death of the Guilds, Professions, States, and the Advance of Capitalism, 1930 to the Present*. New Haven: Yale University Press, 1996.

16 Redesigning the University

1   Pask, Gordon. *Conversation Theory: Applications in Education and Epistemology*. Amsterdam and New York: Elsevier, 1976.

2   Gabriel, Trip. "Live vs. Distance Learning: Measuring the Difference," *New York Times*. November 5, 2010. www.nytimes.com/2010/11/05/us/ 05collegeside.html

3   Eco, Umberto. *Travels in Hyperreality*. Trans. William Weaver. New York: Harcourt Inc., 1986.

4   De Stasio, Elizabeth A., Ansfield, Matthew, Cohen, Paul, and Spurgin, Timothy. "Curricular Responses to 'Electronically Tethered' Students: Individualized Learning Across the Curriculum," *Liberal Education*, vol. 95, no. 4 (Fall 2009). Washington D.C.: Association of American Colleges and Universities, Fall 2009. www.aacu.org/liberaleducation/le- fa09/documents/LE-FA09_IndividLearn.pdf

5   Dewey, John. *Experience and Education*. New York: Macmillan Press, 1938.

6   Martin, Roger. *The Design of Business: Why Design Thinking is the Next Competitive Advantage*. Cambridge, MA: Harvard Business School Publishing, 2009.

17 Fracture-Critical Infrastructure

1   Brinkley, Douglas. *The Great Deluge: Hurricane Katrina, New Orleans, and the Mississippi Gulf Coast*. New York: Harper Collins, 2006.

2   Barron, James. "Power Surge Blacks Out Northeast" *New York Times*, August 15, 2003. www.nytimes.com/2003/08/15/nyregion/15POWE.html? ref=newyorkcityblackoutof2003

3   Williams, Mark. "5 Years After a Giant Blackout, Concerns About Electrical Grid Linger," *The Associated Press*. August 13, 2008. www.mlive. com/business/index.ssf/2008/08/5_years_after_a_giant_blackout.html

4   Hardin, Garrett. "The Tragedy of the Commons," *Science*, vol. 162 (1968): 1243–1248. http://dieoff.org/page95.htm

5   Carl Sagan used the analogy of the atmosphere as a coat of shellac on a basketball-sized earth in the astronomy course I took with him when I was a student at Cornell in the early 1970s.

18 Going Dutch

1   Descartes, René. *A Discourse on Method.* London: Orion Publishing Group, 1994.

2   Schreuder, Yda. "The Polder Model in Dutch Economic and Environmental Planning," *Bulletin of Science, Technology & Society*, vol. 21 (2001): 237. http://bst.sagepub.com/content/21/4/237

3   "Katrina 5 Years Later: The Fall and Rise of New Orleans' Levees," *Newshour*, Public Broadcasting System, August 3, 2010. www.pbs.org/newshour/rundown/2010/08/katrina-5-years-later-the-fall-and-rise-of-new-orleans-levees.html

4   Broad, William. "Taking Lessons from What Went Wrong," *New York Times.* July 19, 2010. www.nytimes.com/2010/07/20/science/20lesson.html?pagewanted=1

5   "Offshore Wind Farm Opens Off the Coast of the Netherlands," *New York Times* April 18, 2007. www.nytimes.com/2007/04/18/business/world business/18iht-wind.4.5338427.html

6   Farrell, John, and Morris, David. *Energy Self-Reliant States, Second and Expanded Edition.* Minneapolis: New Rules Project, 2010. www.new rules.org/energy/publications/energy-selfreliant-states-second-and-expanded-edition

19 Fracture-Critical Developments

1   Jackson, Kenneth T. *Crabgrass Frontier: The Suburbanization of the United States.* New York: Oxford University Press, 1985.

2   McIlwain, John. *Housing in America: The Next Decade.* Washington D.C.: The Urban Land Institute, 2010. www.marc.org/forecast/assets/Housing inAmerica.pdf

3   Bajaj, Vikas, and Leonhardt, David. "Tax Breaks May Have Helped Cause Housing Bubble," *New York Times.* December 18, 2008. www.nytimes.com/2008/12/19/business/19tax.html

4   Andrews, Edmund L. "Fed Shrugged as Subprime Crisis Spread." *New York Times.* December 18, 2007. www.nytimes.com/2007/12/18/business/18subprime.html

5   Yang, Sarah. "Should California consider Australia's Wildfire Policy?" *Berkeleyan.* March 4, 2009. http://berkeley.edu/news/berkeleyan/2009/03/04_Aussiefire.shtml

6   "Two Billion Vulnerable to Floods by 2050; Number Expected to Double or More in Two Generations," *NASA Earth Observatory.* June 13, 2004. http://earthobservatory.nasa.gov/Newsroom/view.php?id=24957

7   Friedman, Lisa. "Bangladesh Endures Ugly Experiments in 'Nature's Laboratory'," *New York Times.* March 9, 2009. http://www.nytimes.com/cwire/2009/03/09/09climatewire-ugly-experiments-in-natures-laboratory-10035.html

8   Campanella, Richard. *Above-Sea-Level New Orleans: The Residential Capacity of Orleans Parish's Higher Ground.* New Orleans: Center for

Bioenvironmental Research, 2007. http:// fleurdelis.tulane.edu/CBR_
Sea-Level_04_07.pdf
9   Locke, Robert. "Marxism of the Right," *The American Conservative.* March
    14, 2005. http://www.amconmag.com/article/2005/mar/14/00017/

20 A Better Way to Dwell

1   Rossignol, Jacqueline, and Wandsnider, LuAnn (eds.). *Space, Time, and
    Archaeological Landscapes.* New York: Plenum Press, 1992.
2   West, Geoffrey. "Why the Future of Humanity and the Long-term
    Sustainability of the Planet are Inextricably Linked to the Fate of our
    Cities," *Seed.* July 5, 2010. http://seedmagazine.com/content/article/
    urban_paradox/
3   Ibid.
4   Ibid.
5   Ibid.
6   Smith, Adam. *The Theory of Moral Sentiments.* New York: Penguin
    Classics, 2010, pp. 184–185.
7   Cohen, Joel. *How Many People Can the Earth Support?* New York: Norton,
    1996.
8   Thoreau, Henry David. *Walden, or Life in the Woods.* Boston: Beacon
    Press, 2004.

21 Fracture-Critical Buildings

1   Interlandi, Jeneen. "Why the Palace Fell," *Newsweek.* January 21, 2010.
    www.newsweek.com/2010/01/20/why-the-palace-fell.html
2   Bachelor, Rosemary E. "World's 20 Most Earthquake Prone Cities,"
    Natural Disasters@suite101. March 6, 2010. www.suite101.com/content/
    worlds-20-most-earthquake-prone-cities-a209850
3   "Report Card of America's Infrastructure," American Society of Civil
    Engineers. www.infrastructurereportcard.org/
4   Cheung, Moe, Foo, Simon, and Granadino, Jacques. "Seismic Retrofit of
    Existing Buildings: Innovative Alternatives," Public Works & Government
    Services Canada. www.icomos.org/iiwc/seismic/Cheung-M.pdf
5   Glanz, James. "Towers Believed to Be Safe Proved Vulnerable to an
    Intense Jet Fuel Fire, Experts Say," *New York Times.* September 12, 2001.
    www.nytimes.com/2001/09/12/us/day-terror-buildings-towers-believed-
    be-safe-proved-vulnerable-intense-jet-fuel.html?src=pm
6   "Soddy," Ramsey County Historical Society. http://www.rchs.com/Gibbs
    %20Museum%20Pioneer%20Soddy.htm
7   "Why," Architecture 2030. http://architecture2030.org/the_problem/
    buildings_problem_why
8   "Native American Houses" Native Languages. http://www.native-
    languages.org/houses.htm.
9   Trilling, Lionel. *The Liberal Imagination.* New York: New York Review of
    Books, 2008.

22 Designing for Durability

1 Someya, Satoshi. "The Role of R&D in Construction Firms." Masters Thesis, Civil Engineering, MIT, June 1992. dspace.mit.edu/bitstream/handle/1721.1/45724/27352366.pdf
2 Prowler, Don, and Treschsel, Heinz. "Mold and Moisture Dynamics," *Whole Building Design Guide*. National Institute of Building Sciences, Washington D.C., June, 15, 2010. http://www.wbdg.org/resources/moisturedynamics.php
3 Hansen, Kristin A. "Geographical Mobility," Population Profile of the United States. U.S. Census Bureau. http://www.census.gov/population/www/pop-profile/geomob.html
4 "Before You Specify, Before You Build . . ." *Sustainability/Residential Wall Systems Comparison Tool*, Georgia Pacific. http://www.gp.com/build/BPContent.aspx?elementId=10170&repository=bp
5 Jackson, Mike. "Embodied Energy and Historic Preservation: A Needed Reassessment," *APT Bulletin: Journal of Preservation Technology*, vol. 36, no. 3 (2005). www.ironwarrior.org/ARE/Materials_Methods/EmbodHP.pdf

23 Fracture-Critical Consumption

1 Max-Neef, Manfred, and Ekins, Paul (eds.). *Real-Life Economics: Understanding Wealth Creation*. London: Routledge, 1992.
2 Ibid.
3 "Making Better Energy Choices," *Worldwatch Institute*, August 9, 2011. www.worldwatch.org/node/808
4 "Sustainabilty, Carrying Capacity, and Overconsumption," *World Overpopulation Awareness*, August 9, 2011. http://www.overpopulation.org/solutions.html
5 Ignatieff, Michael. *The Needs of Strangers*. New York: Picador, 1984.
6 Schwartz, Barry. *The Paradox of Choice: Why More is Less*. New York: Harper Perennial, 2004.
7 Kahneman, Daniel, and Deaton, Angus. "High Income Improves Evaluation of Life, but Not Emotional Well-Being," *Proceedings of the National Academy of Sciences*. September 7, 2010. www.pnas.org/content/early/2010/08/27/1011492107
8 Vivenza, Gloria. *Adam Smith and the Classics: The Classical Heritage of Adam Smith's Thought*. Oxford: Oxford University Press, 2001.

24 Creative Citizen Consumption

1 Maslow, Abraham H. *Motivation and Personality*. New York: Harper, 1943.
2 Cohen, Lizabeth. *A Consumers' Republic: The Politics of Mass Consumption in Postwar America*. New York: Vintage Books, 2003.
3 Came, Daniel. "Nietzsche on Ethics and Aesthetics," in *Nietzsche on Art and Life*. Oxford: Oxford University Press, 2011. http://oxford.academia.edu/DanielCame/Papers/377070/Nietzsche_on_Ethics_and_Aesthetics

25 Why We Have So Much Bad Design

1   Ben-David, Itzhak, Graham, John R., and Harvey, Campbell R. "Managerial Overconfidence and Corporate Policies." http://ideas.repec.org/p/nbr/nberwo/13711.html

2   Ibid.

3   Albert, Stuart. *When? The Art of Timing.* Boston: Harvard Business School Press, 2010. http://hbr.org/product/when-the-art-of-timing/an/2652-HBK-ENG

4   Amadeo, Kimberly. "Dodd Frank Wall Street Reform Act." http://useconomy.about.com/od/criticalissues/p/Dodd-Frank-Wall-Street-Reform-Act.htm

5   Panek, Richard. *The Invisible Century: Einstein, Freud, and the Search for Hidden Universes.* New York: Viking Penguin, 2005.

6   Martin, Roger, and Dunne, David. "Design Thinking and How It Will Change Management Education: An Interview and Discussion," *Academy of Management Learning & Education,* vol. 5, no. 4 (2006): 512–523. www.rotman.utoronto.ca/rogermartin/AcademyofManagementLearning.pdf

7   Pink, Daniel. *A Whole New Mind: Moving from the Information Age to the Conceptual Age.* New York: Riverhead Books, 2005.

8   Coxon, Gareth. "Business: Great design can increase business – Design Council research." November 29, 2008. www.ecademy.com/node.php?id=117494

26 The Design Mind

1   "What is Design?" London: Design Council, 2002. www.hku.hk/bse/interdisciplinary/what_is_design.pdf

2   Senge, Peter. "The Leader's New Work: Building Learning Organizations," *Sloan Management Review,* vol. 32, no. 1 (Fall 1990). www.nationalqualitycenter.org/download_resource.cfm?fileID=38439

3   Wapnick, Adelle. "Introducing the Design Economy," *Marketing Web,* September 26, 2007. www.marketingweb.co.za/marketingweb/view/marketingweb/en/page71654?oid=95196&sn=Marketingweb detail

4   Breen, Bill. "Masters of Design," *Fast Company.* June 1, 2004. www.fastcompany.com/magazine/83/mod.html

5   Whitney, Patrick. "Business Design: The New Competitive Weapon," Live@Rotman: MBA Business Conference 2005. www.rotman.utoronto.ca/businessdesign/file/conference2.pdf

6   Nussbaum, Bruce. "Redesigning American Business," *Business Week.* November 29, 2004. www.businessweek.com/print/bwdaily/dnflash/nov2004/nf20041129_2629.htm?chan=db&

7   Zapolski, John. In "Perspectives on Design + Strategy," 2005 Institute of Design Strategy Conference, Institute of Design, IIT, 2005. www.id.iit.edu/141/getdocument.php?id=71

8   Quoted in Senge, Peter. *The Fifth Discipline: The Art and Practice of the Learning Organization.* New York: Doubleday, 1990.

9 Dumas, Angla, and Mintzberg, Henry. "Managing the Form, Function, and Fit of Design," *DMI Review*, vol. 2, no. 3 (Summer 1991). www.dmi.org/dmi/html/publications/journal/fullabstract_d.jsp?itemID=9123DUM26

10 Webster, Rudi. "Bennett King: Celebration or Disaster." *Caribbean Cricket*. http://caribbeancricket.com/news/0000/00/00/2047

27 The Process of Design

1 Farson, Richard. *The Power of Design: A Force for Transforming Everything*. Norcross, GA: Ostberg Library of Design Management, 2008.

2 Simon, Herbert. *The Sciences of the Artificial*. Cambridge, MA: MIT Press, 1996.

3 Quoted from an address that she gave to the Association of Collegiate Schools of Architecture, Administrators Conference, Savannah, Georgia, 2008.

4 Aristotle. *Metaphysics*. Chicago: Great Books of the Western World, Vol. 8. University of Chicago Press, 1952.

5 Plato. *Dialogues, The Republic*. Chicago: Great Books of the Western World, Vol. 7., University of Chicago Press. 1952.

6 "Young Drivers: The Road to Safety," *Policy Brief*. Organization for Economic Co-operation and Development, October 2006. www.internationaltransportforum.org/jtrc/safety/YDpolicyBrief.pdf

28 The Logic of Design

1 Gardner, Howard. *Frames of Mind: The Theory of Multiple Intelligences*. New York: Basic Books, 2004.

2 "Inductive Logic," *Stanford Encyclopedia of Philosophy*. June 20, 2011. http://plato.stanford.edu/entries/logic-inductive/

3 "Abduction," *Stanford Encyclopedia of Philosophy*. March 9, 2011. http://plato.stanford.edu/entries/abduction/

29 The Pragmatics of Design

1 "Charles Sanders Peirce," *Stanford Encyclopedia of Philosophy*. August 3, 2010. http://plato.stanford.edu/ entries/peirce/

2 Shank, Gary, and Cunningham, Donald J. "Modeling the Six Modes of Peircean Abduction for Educational Purposes." www.cs.indiana.edu/event/maics96/Proceedings/shank.html

3 Ibid.

4 Fann, K.T. *Peirce's Theory of Abduction*. The Hague: Martinusnijhoff, 1970. www.dca.fee.unicamp.br

5 "Firstness." http://www.helsinki.fi/science/commens/terms/firstness.html

30 The Holon of Design

1 Koestler, Arthur. *The Ghost in the Machine.* New York: Macmillan, 1968.
2 Ibid.
3 Kant, Immanuel. *Groundwork for the Metaphysics of Morals.* New Haven: Yale University Press, 2002.
4 Smith. *The Theory of Moral Sentiments.*
5 Najafizada, Enayat, and Nordland, Rod. "Afghans Avenge Florida Koran Burning, Killing 12," *New York Times*, April 1, 2011. www.nytimes.com/2011/04/02/world/asia/02afghanistan.html?pagewanted=all

31 Designing Our Future

1 William Rees gave the talk at the 2007 convention of the American Institute of Architects in San Antonio, Texas.
2 Judt, Tony. "Europe vs. America," *New York Review of Books.* February 10, 2005: p. 39. www.nybooks.com/articles/archives/2005/feb/10/europe-vs-america/
3 Farson, Richard. "Is Architecture as Important as Education?" a talk given at the AIA Board Meeting, 2003.
4 Ibid.
5 John Cary, one of the founders of the movement, has a blog by that name: Public Interest Design, www.publicinterestdesign.org/
6 Emanuel, Kerry. *Divine Wind: The History and Science of Hurricanes.* Oxford: Oxford University Press, 2006.
7 Myers, Norman. "Environmental Refugees in a Globally Warmed World," *Bioscience*, vol. 43, no. 11 (December 1993). www.jstor.org/pss/1312319
8 "We Can End Poverty: 2015 Millennium Development Goals." New York: United Nations. www.un.org/millenniumgoals.
9 This was designed as part of a design studio at the College of Design, University of Minnesota. www.youtube.com/watch?v=eovZMtvZPlE
10 There are few organizations that have done more than Architecture for Humanity to launch the public-interest design movement globally and to engage the design community in the needs of the 90 percent of the world's population without access to design services. http://www.architectureforhumanity.org
11 The conference that Bryan Bell and Design Corps founded, Structures for Inclusion, has also become a major annual event, gathering the diverse groups of architects and designers working on behalf of impoverished people. www.designcorps.org/
12 The Margaret Mead statement "Never doubt that a small group of thoughtful, committed citizens can change the world" applies to groups like Public Architecture, who, with very few funds, have started a national movement that has done tremendous good. www.publicarchitecture.org/
13 Kroeker, Richard. *Richard Kroeker Design.* www.richardkroekerdesign.com/

14   Janz, Wes. *OneSmallProject*. http://archinect.com/navigate/35227/http% 253A%252F%252Fwww.onesmallproject.com%252F

32 What We Can Live Without

1   Hobbes, Thomas. *Leviathan.* Chicago: Great Books of the Western World, Vol. 23. University of Chicago Press, 1952.
2   Rousseau, Jean-Jacques. *The Social Contract.* Chicago: Great Books of the Western World, Vol. 38. University of Chicago Press, 1952.
3   Thoreau. *Walden.*
4   "World Population to 2300," United Nations Department of Economic and Social Affairs, Population Division. www.un.org/esa/population/ publications/longrange2/WorldPop2300final.pdf
5   Dean, Andrea Oppenheimer, and Hursley, Timothy. *Rural Studio: Samuel Mockbee and an Architecture of Decency.* New York: Princeton Architectural Press, 2002.
6   Sorkin, Michael. *Michael Sorkin Studio.* http://sorkinstudio.net/Index. htm
7   Dutton, Thomas. "Miami University, Center for Community Engagement in Over the Rhine." http://arts.muohio.edu/cce/residency_program.html
8   Shi, David. *The Simple Life: Plain Living and High Thinking in American Culture.* New York: Oxford University Press, 1985.
9   Chapin, Ross. *Pocket Neighborhoods: Creating Small-Scale Community in a Large-Scale World.* Newtown, CT: Taunton Press, 2011.
10   Shi. *The Simple Life.*
11   A statement made by Philippe Starck at a lecture he gave at the Walker Art Center in Minneapolis. www.starck.com/en/
12   Frank, Robert. *Falling Behind: How Rising Inequality Harms the Middle Class.* Berkeley: University of California Press, 2007.

33 The Adulthood of the Species

1   Fuller, Steve. *The Sociology of Intellectual Life.* London: Sage Publications, 2009.
2   Dickens, Charles. *Martin Chuzzlewit.* London: Penguin Books, 1999.
3   Fuller. *The Sociology of Intellectual Life.*
4   Observations made by professor John Koepke, a Native American colleague in the Department of Landscape Architecture at the University of Minnesota.
5   When you "Google" the word "design," you find far more comes up for the intelligent design argument against evolution than for anything related to human design activities.
6   Deleuze, Gilles, and Guattari, Felix. *Anti-Oedipus, Capitalism and Schizophrenia.* New York: Continuum, 2004.

34 Media, Metaphor, and Meaning

1   McLuhan. *The Gutenberg Galaxy*.
2   Birkeland, Janis. *Design for Sustainability: A Sourcebook of Integrated, Ecological Solutions*. London: Earthscan Publications, 2002.
3   Capra, Fritjof. *The Web of Life: A New Understanding of Living Systems*. New York: Anchor Books, 1996.
4   Dutta, Prajit. *Strategies and Games: Theory and Practice*. Cambridge, MA: MIT Press, 1999.
5   Jacobs, Jane. *The Economy of Cities*. New York: Random House, 1969.
6   Illich, Ivan. *ABC: The Alphabetization of the Popular Mind*. San Francisco: North Point Press, 1988.
7   Leadbeater, Charles. *The Weightless Society: Living in the New Economy Bubble*. New York: Texere, 2000.
8   Rifkin. *The End of Work*.
9   Horwitz, Morton. *The Transformation of American Law, 1870–1960*. New York: Oxford University Press, 1992.
10 Mallgrave, Henry Francis, and Contandriopoulos, Christina (eds.). *Architectural Theory, Volume II: An Anthology from 1871–2005*. Malden, MA: Blackwell Publishing, 2008.

35 The Nature of Things to Come

1   Zimmern, Alfred Eckhard. *The Prospects of Democracy and other Essays*. London: Chatto & Windus, 1929.
2   Quarantelli, Enrico. *What is a Disaster? Perspectives on the Question*. New York: Routledge, 1998.
3   Clarke, Lee. *Worst Cases: Terror and Catastrophe in the Popular Imagination*. Chicago: University of Chicago Press, 2006.
4   This quote is attributed to Albert Einstein, although when he said it remains unclear, at least to me.
5   Bloch, Arthur. *Murphy's Law and Other Reasons Why Things Go Wrong*. London: Methuen, 1977.
6   Solnit, Rebecca. *A Paradise Built in Hell: The Extraordinary Communities that Arise in Disaster*. New York: Viking Penguin, 2009.
7   Epictetus. *Enchiridion*. Amherst, NY: Prometheus Books, 1991.
8   Rawls, John. *A Theory of Justice*. Cambridge, MA: Harvard University Press, 1971.
9   Solnit. *A Paradise Built in Hell*.

36 Hell or Paradise?

1   Solnit. *A Paradise Built in Hell*.
2   Ibid.
3   McKibben, Bill. *Eaarth: Making a Life on a Tough New Planet*. New York: Henry Holt, 2010.

4   West, Geoffrey. "The Universal Scale of Life," *Thought Leader Forum*. 2002. www.capatcolumbia.com/CSFB%20TLF/2002/west_sidecolumn.pdf

5   Lehrer, Jonah. "A Physicist Solves the City," *New York Times*. December 19, 2010. www.nytimes.com/2010/12/19/magazine/19Urban_West-t.html?pagewanted=all

6   McKibben, Bill. *The Age of Missing Information*. New York: Plume Penguin, 1993.

Illustration Credits

26.1   John Dwyer
26.2   Metropolitan Design Center Image Bank. © Regents of the University
        of Minnesota. All rights reserved. Used with permission
27.1   John Dwyer
27.2   Kamana Dhakhwa
27.3   Kamana Dhakhwa
28.1   Kamana Dhakhwa
28.2   Kamana Dhakhwa
29.1   Kamana Dhakhwa
30.1   Kamana Dhakhwa
30.2   Kamana Dhakhwa
31.1   John Dwyer
31.2   Architecture for Humanity
31.3   Bryan Bell, Design Corps
31.4   Public Architecture
31.5   Richard Kroeker
31.6   Kevin Klinger
32.1   Rural Studio
32.2   Ross Chapin
36.1   Kamana Dhakhwa

Index